Luck, Chance or Prayer

The Basics of Prayer

ILYNMW Publishing
Atlanta Georgia

Dedication

This book is dedicated to my Bride and the love of my life - Debbie. God has been so gracious to me in giving me a best friend who is by my side no matter what.

In addition, I want to dedicate this book to my children - Hannah, David, Sarah and Jonathan. I am so proud of you guys and I love you no matter what!

Cover Design: Paul Beersdorf

ISBN 978-0-9983413-3-0

"Scripture taken from the NEW AMERICAN STANDARD BIBLE®, Copyright © 1960,1962,1963,1968,1971,1972,1973,1975,1977,1995 by The Lockman Foundation. Used by permission."

Books by Paul Beersdorf

Flowers on Tuesday

The 100 Most Important Words

Encouraging Your Wife

Encouraging Your Husband

Advice for Today, Tomorrow and Forever

Even Moses Needed Encouragement

Storm Management

Living Intentionally

Choosing to Finish Well

Contents

Acknowledgments	Page 6
Preface	Page 7
Introduction	Page 8
What is Prayer	Page 12
George's Prayers	Page 14
God's Concern	Page 16
Being The Answer	Page 18
Answered Prayers	Page 25
Continual Prayer	Page 38
Why Pray	Page 43
When to Pray	Page 61
Where to Pray	Page 65
Posture of Prayer	Page 70
Prayer Recap	Page 74
A.C.T.S.	Page 75
Types of Prayer	Page 81
Barriers to Prayer	Page 88
Paul's Call to Pray	Page 93
Prayer by the Numbers	Page 106
Famous Prayers	Page 111
Prayer Quotes	Page 112
Jesus as the example	Page 114
Perfect Prayer	Page 120
How not to pray	Page 123
Asking	Page 127
Fasting	Page 132
Praying for Church Leaders and Missionaries	Page 138
Final Thoughts	Page 145
Study Lessons	Page 146

Acknowledgments

I love my Beautiful Bride and how much she encourages me to write and share my thoughts and ideas. She is the love of my life and my best friend. Nothing I do would be worthwhile without her by my side.

Preface

To be clear, I am no Bible scholar or professor. I have never been to seminary and offer no credentials as a pastor, preacher or evangelist. I only offer my credentials as a follower of Christ for over 40 years.

This book is not designed to be an in depth study of prayer (there are plenty of those done by people much more qualified than myself). The design of this book is to offer the topic of prayer to those who are curious from a layman's perspective and want to dig a little deeper into the subject.

I wanted to learn much more about prayer and started an in-depth study of the subject. I then went a step further and prepared a Sunday School lesson about prayer and then used that material as the impetus for this book.

If nothing else, I have increased my own knowledge of prayer and hope to put that knowledge to practical use.

My hope and prayer is that you would be encouraged by this book and have a deeper desire to know more about prayer, an improved prayer life and an appreciation for the power of prayer.

Blessing to you as you read this book.

Introduction

"Don't pray when you feel like it. Have an appointment with the Lord and keep it. A man is powerful on his knees."
Corrie Ten Boom

This is a book about prayer; the who, what, when, where, why and how of prayer. It is also a book about answered prayers, and being an answer to prayer.

I have had this book on my heart for some time and I have been ..... you guessed it, praying about what to say and how to say it with the written word.

It has been several months since I have had an opportunity to even think about writing. My "day job" has been unbelievably busy – to the point of working nights and weekends (something I am loath to do). However, I finally caught a break in the action and was able to finish this book over the Christmas holidays.

In my own life as a young believer, prayer was something that was hit or miss for me. I was not raised in a Christian home, so there was no example of prayer of praying in my family. It was only after I married my beautiful Bride that I got much more serious about prayer. In fact, when I reached a significant age milestone, my prayer life became much more real to me. Also, being a father of four children increased my need and desire to pray.

I have found while it is very gratifying and satisfying to have a prayer answered, it is much more fulfilling to be an answer to the prayer of others. That is when you get to see the true hand of God at work.

The stories in this book are mostly from our family's life and experience. I thought it would be more useful to relate our stories with prayer in our life, than rehashing stories you may have heard before. Additionally, I have first-hand knowledge of all the prayers in our life and do not have to wonder if the story is a work of fiction or wild imagination.

I leave it to you the reader to either believe or not each of the stories in this book. Some stories may seem trivial, and others more serious, but in the end, I want God to receive the honor and glory He so richly deserves.

Finally, you can also decide for yourself if it was Luck, Chance or Prayer that was involved in each of these stories. As a Christian, I do not believe in luck or chance. I believe in God and the power of prayer. I have seen the evidence in my life and the life of my family and do not need to consider the world view of happenstance or serendipity.

Prayer is not something that should be done in a hap hazardous way. It can and should be done in an intentional and deliberate way. Now that does not mean there are times when we will cry out to God in the stress and pain of a sudden storm in our life. Certainly we would want to plead and make our petitions know in those desperate times. However, for most of us, those distressing times are few and far between.

Therefore being intentional about your prayer life is critical not only for those who you are praying for, but also for your own relationship with the Lord and daily communion with Him.

The other goal of our prayer life is to be an example for our children and to lead them in paths of righteousness and to teach them how to pray by watching mom and dad praying.

With our children we have been following the same process for years.

1. In the mornings before school, my Beautiful Bride gathers all of the children and they have their devotion and prayer time together that she leads. It is a very sweet time together and a great way to start the day. They have many different people and situations they are praying for and the prayer list is constantly changing as needs change.

2. In the evenings we gather all of the children again in our bedroom and I lead the family in prayer as we end the day. Here are a few of the intentional things I always pray for:

    a. Wisdom and Discernment
    b. Keep my children close and clean (mind, body, soul)
    c. Keep me close and clean
    d. Pray for my children's future spouse (my Daughter Hannah is 25 and I have been praying for her husband since I knew she was a baby girl in her mother's womb)
    e. Pray that the fruits of the spirit would be evident in our life (Love, Joy, Peace, Patience, Kindness, Goodness, Faithfulness, Gentleness and Self-Control.
    f. Thankfulness for the food, clothing and shelter God provides
    g. Thankfulness for the gift of Salvation through Christ Jesus
    h. We end with the Lord's Prayer

3. We always pray at every meal, whether it is at home or in public. We are giving thanks to God for the food and for those with us at the meal.

For myself I have a prayer journal that I keep and use to record my prayer requests and the on-going list of people I am praying for. All of my favorite Bible verses are also recorded in this journal for quick reference.

My prayer list includes:

- My Beautiful Bride
- My Children
- My extended family
- Close Friends
- Our Pastor
- Missionaries
- My co-workers
- My boss
- Any special needs or urgent prayer requests
- Finally – myself.

Here are the things I continually pray for myself. This is my constant list that has varied little over time.

- ✓ Wisdom
- ✓ Discernment
- ✓ Keep me close and clean
- ✓ Finishing Well
- ✓ Leading an intentional life
- ✓ Right Attitude
- ✓ Contentment
- ✓ That I would be a dream maker and not a dream taker
- ✓ That I would be an encourager
- ✓ That the fruits of the spirit would be evident in my life (Love, Joy, Peace, Patience, Kindness, Goodness, Faithfulness, Gentleness and Self-Control

These things have been and will continue to be on my prayer list for the rest of my life.   Therefore, if you feel compelled to pray for me, then you have a handy list right here.

Whenever someone asks me how they can pray for me, I almost always give them my short list – Wisdom, Discernment and Right Attitude.   All of the issues in my life would be much better if I had these three things.

When I tell someone I am going to pray for them, I do it right then. I don't wait until later, I pray right at that moment. I don't want to get busy and forget to pray for them.

I have one lady who has been battling breast cancer for over 15 years, and she has been on my prayer list all these years.   I continue to pray for healing, recovery and hope.

It is important to remember people in prayer who are dealing with long term challenges like cancer or other debilitating illnesses.   Many people will come alongside them early in the challenge but life is a marathon and not a sprint.   It is critical to continue to encourage them and continually lift them in prayer.

Remember, prayer is not a sometime thing, it is an all the time thing. Pray without ceasing.

What is Prayer?

Let's start with the very basic question – "What is prayer?" Here is a very clinical definition from Merriam-Webster:

Definition of prayer (Merriam-Webster)

A. an address (such as a petition) to God or a god in word or thought
B. an earnest request or wish

So prayer is most easily defined as a conversation or request to God. This conversation can be verbalized – out loud, or it can be a thought in our heart and mind. Either way, the most basic answer is that prayer is just a conversation with God. You can have this conversation with God anywhere (public or private), anytime (24/7/365) and you can have the conversation in any language.

To be clear, prayer is not a passive activity (as no real conversation is a passive activity). When praying, approach God with reverence and honor but talk to Him as a friend. Abraham was called a "friend of God", so you too can talk to God as a friend – meaning you do not have to use fancy words or phrases, you do not have to be eloquent or even prepared, you can simply have an open and honest conversation.

James 2:23

and the Scripture was fulfilled which says, "And Abraham believed God, and it was reckoned to him as righteousness," and he was called the friend of God.

You may be thinking you should not bother God with prayer, but the bible also instructs us to call upon God in prayer and He will be listening.

Jeremiah 29:12-13

Then you will call upon Me and come and pray to Me, and I will listen to you. You will seek Me and find Me when you search for Me with all your heart.

Psalm 91:15

"He will call upon Me, and I will answer him;
I will be with him in trouble;
I will rescue him and honor him.

Isaiah 65:24

It will also come to pass that before they call, I will answer; and while they are still speaking, I will hear.

Matthew 7:7

Ask, and it will be given to you; seek, and you will find; knock, and it will be opened to you.

I know this seems too basic and simple to be true, but prayer really is that simple. It is about a conversation between you and God. I encourage you to have a robust and healthy dialog with God each and every day. He is always waiting and watching for your prayers, supplication and petitions.

As you start reading this book, make the commitment to make prayer a part of your daily routine. Commit all of your endeavors to prayer and make prayer a part of your very DNA, such that it permeates all that you say and do each and every day.

My prayer right now is that God will deeply bless you as you read this book and give you some new understanding and wisdom in regards to prayer and praying.

George's Prayers

James 5:16

.... The effective prayer of a righteous man can accomplish much.

George Mueller is one of my modern heroes of the faith. He was a man who completely trusted God for his provision and needs and ministered to the orphans of England during the 1800's.

His orphanages served over 10,000 children and yet he never made the needs of the orphanage known to anyone. During his lifetime he had over 50,000 prayers answered. They only reason we know about these answered prayers is because he would give an annual account of the orphanage and tell of Gods great provision – after the fact.

There are so many incredible stories of answers to George's prayers. Here are just a few for you to consider.

Breakfast for hundreds

One morning the children in the orphanage awoke for breakfast and there was no food to be found in the entire house. Over 300 children did not know what they would eat that morning. George had them all sit down and they prayed and thanked God for the meal they were about to receive. They then waited upon the Lord.

It did not take long! A baker showed up with enough loaves of bread (having be prompted by God the night before in a dream to bake the bread for the children) and then later a milk cart broke down in front of the orphanage and all the milk was given to the children.

Every day George would pray, and God would provide. Not only did God provide for the orphans all those years, God also gave George the desires of his heart as well.

Missionary

George had always wanted to be a missionary and share the Good News of the Gospel of Jesus. When George was 70 years old he became a missionary and did this work for 17 years! He traveled to 42 countries and was God's messenger of the gospel. What an incredible man to venture out into the world at age 70 and be used by God.

Lifting the Fog

One of my favorite stories of answered prayer is when George was on a ship headed to America and a thick fog would cause a delay such that George would miss his appointment. The captain of the ship told him there was no way through the fog, and George told him God would find a way through. He and the captain went below and prayed the fog would be lifted and they could continue their journey. When they emerged from below, the fog was gone! What is amazing about this story is that George never told this story. It was told by the captain (who did not really believe the fog would be lifted to begin with).

I would encourage you to take the time to learn about the life and times of George Mueller and how he was a faithful servant of God and how God consistently met the need.

God's Concern

Luke 12:6-7

Are not five sparrows sold for two cents? Yet not one of them is forgotten before God. Indeed, the very hairs of your head are all numbered. Do not fear; you are more valuable than many sparrows.

God is concerned about all aspects of your life. Not just the big concerns. Too often we put God in a small box that says "Break In Case of Emergency" and then we forget about God as we struggle and strain with the everyday cares of life because we think God is not concerned about them. Or perhaps you say something like "I don't want to disturb God with this little thing, He is much too busy".

In the verse above, the Bible makes it very clear that God is concerned about ALL things. He considers the very sparrows of the air or hairs on your head (although I am bald, so this does not apply to me). When you consider sparrows, they are small birds that seemingly go unnoticed and uncared for, and yet God provides the air they breathe, the trees to nest upon, the food to eat, the sunshine for warmth and so much more. You are made in the VERY image of God, he cares so much more for you.

The context of this verse was about not being fearful, but I would tell you not to be fearful to bring your prayers and petitions to God.

1 Peter 5:7

casting all your anxiety on Him, because He cares for you

Psalm 55:22

Cast your burden upon the Lord and He will sustain you;
He will never allow the righteous to be shaken.

The term casting would be familiar to fisherman who would cast nets into the ocean to capture fish.   When you cast a wide net, you capture both the big things and the little things.   Everything is swept into the net.   In this case, by casting your burdens upon God, your net goes out empty, but God Himself fills the net with everything you need, when you need it (and at times he also goes beyond your needs and blesses you with more). Sometimes the net will come back empty, but you keep on casting. Your casting is an act of faith and we know God is faithful.   We do not always understand the empty net, but we do understand God always has our best interest in mind.

Philippians 4:6

Be anxious for nothing, but in everything by prayer and supplication with thanksgiving let your requests be made known to God.

In the preceding three verses you can see how the Bible calls us to cast **ALL** or EVERYTHING upon the Lord. It does not say to limit it to only the BIG things.   God is concerned about all things in our life. I looked up the word "All" and" Everything" in the Greek to make sure I understood the actual word. Do you know what it means in the Greek? It means ALL!

You have to believe this in your, heart, mind, body and soul if you are going to bring **All** your prayers and petitions to God.

Finally, consider this verse:

John 3:16

"For God so loved the world, that He gave His only begotten Son, that whoever believes in Him shall not perish, but have eternal life.

God's concern not only extends to the utter most parts of this world, it extends to eternity.   He loved us so much, He made the ultimate sacrifice.

God loves you!
God cares for you!
God wants to hear from you!

As you read the next few chapters, ask God to open your heart and mind and consider how you will approach Him in your prayer life.

Being the Answer

"We make a living by what we get, but we make a life by what we give."
Winston Churchill

I can tell you from personal experience, that it is as much a blessing to be an answer to a prayer for someone else, as it is to have a prayer answered. We have been very blessed in our marriage to be the answer to other people's prayers.   It is always incredible to see how God works and chooses to use us as instruments of His glory.   Our faith is always increased as is the faith of the person whose prayer is answered as well as those who get to hear the story.

I hope as you read the following stories, you will be blessed and encouraged and know the God of this universe loves you and is concerned about all aspects of your life.

The Mailbox

Several years ago, there was a young lady in our church (we will call her Mary) and she felt called to go on her very first short-term mission trip. We knew her and her family and they are friends of ours.

Mary sent us a letter asking for our financial and prayer support for her mission trip.

Now usually, I like to immediately respond with a letter and a check because I want to be the first to encourage those who are stepping out on faith and heading out to share the Good News of the Gospel of Jesus.

For some reason, I got distracted and the letter got lost on the desk in my office (which at times can be unbelievably cluttered and disorganized).

A few weeks passed and I was cleaning up my desk and found the letter. I was somewhat embarrassed at my forgetfulness and quickly wrote out a check and put the letter in the mail and promptly forgot about the whole episode.

Several days later my Bride called me at work. She was so excited and could not wait to tell me what had happened. She had just received a call from Mary's mother who was in tears (of joy) and praising God.

Mary's mother had gone that afternoon to pick up Mary from school and when Mary got in the car, she just broke down and cried. Her mother wanted to know what was wrong and Mary told her she had a meeting that evening at church for the mission trip and if she did not have her minimum deposit amount available that night, then she would not be able to go on the trip. She felt certain God had called her to go on this trip, but could not understand why she had not received any financial support. She had mailed plenty of support letters to friends and family but nobody had replied. She had been faithfully praying and seeking God during this time, but was visibly upset.

Her mother wisely pulled the car over and they talked for a bit and then her mother prayed the following prayer "Lord, if you want Mary to go on this mission trip, we are trusting you to provide the resources and know you can and will do that. We love you Lord and praise you for all you do for us".

They then drove the rest of the way home.

When they pulled up to the house, Mary jumped out and ran to the mail box and there was one letter in the box. It was the letter I had sent.

Mary had not asked for a specific amount of money, she had only asked for any type of financial support.   However, the check I wrote was for the EXACT amount she need for the deposit that evening.

You see, God's timing is so much better than ours. If I had sent the letter when I was "supposed" to, then Mary would have received her check many weeks earlier and she would not have had the opportunity to have her faith increased.   God multiplied Mary's faith, her mother's faith and our faith with the opportunity.   I can tell you that the joy of being an answer to this young ladies prayer is one of the greatest gifts in life.

To give intentionally, means to always being open for the opportunities to give and looking for those opening when you can be generous to others.

The Pantry

Here is a slightly different story that happened very early in my marriage.

When my Bride and I were first married, we needed to buy some groceries, and since a brand new Wal-Mart Supercenter had just been built in my hometown, we decided to go there. Now you need to know that I do all the grocery shopping for our family. I know that is unusual, but I really enjoy grocery shopping. I have my list and know what we need.

However, on this occasion, we decided to LOAD up! It was a new store and they had some great prices, so I just started throwing things in the basket. My Bride was exploring other parts of the store while I went up and down every grocery aisle.

It was just the two of us at that time (no kids yet), but I had an overflowing basket of food.

As we stood in line, I looked at my Bride and told her, "This food is not for us, I think we need to take this to my grandparents' house and give it to them".   Now, I had not talked to my parents or grandparents for a number of weeks, so I had no idea why they might need the food, therefore I just concluded that the prompting in my heart came from God.

To my Bride's credit she said that sounded like a great surprise and a chance to catch up with my grandparents.

We drove to their house and nobody was home. This was very curious indeed (they were almost always home).

We slipped into the house and filled up the refrigerator and pantry with all the food and beverages and left. We did not leave a note, nor did we tell anyone what we did. It was our little secret.

A few days later, my father called me and wanted to know if we were the ones who had dropped off all the food at my grandparents' house. They had been calling everyone to see who had done it. Since we did not live that close by we were the last ones they called.

I confessed that it was us and my father was stunned. He wanted to know how we knew what to buy? I told him it was just a surprise and we felt like we should give the food to Granny and Granddaddy. He still wanted to know how we knew what was on their grocery list.

You see, they had made out a grocery list and were prepared to go shopping and them my grandfather got sick and they had to rush him to the hospital. That is why nobody was home. My grandparents had spent their last money for that month on the hospital visit and medicine and did not know what they were going to do about food. However, my grandmother was a godly woman who prayed and she knew God would supply the need somehow.

The need was supplied by her grandson. I love how we were able to meet a need for my grandparents and increase their faith and our own. God is so very good all the time.

It is important to look for the opportunities to give and be ready to meet the needs of others. It is important to let your heart be ready to be prompted by God and moved to do things that you might not completely understand but have the potential to bless others and bring honor and glory to God.

Cars

When I graduated from college I was blessed to receive a company car so I did not need my current car. I married my Beautiful Bride and she had her own car, so it was two of us and three cars. We prayed about who to donate the car to, but we were just not sure who should get the car.

Unbeknownst to us there was a man by the name of Tom Young who had a ministry that worked with missionaries going onto the mission field and returning home on furlough. We knew him only slightly as a member of our church.

That week Tom was working with some missionaries who were going to be on furlough and would need a car to travel around the USA.

They started praying for a car and made their request know to God. Time passed and still no car

Finally, the day came when they boarded the plane for a 12 hour trip to the USA and still had no car, but they were trusting God. They were literally traveling on a wing and a prayer.

Sometime that day, while they were in the air, I called up Tom Young and told him I had a car to donate and did he know anybody who could use a car? We had been praying about it and decided to call him for some advice. Of course Tom knew somebody who could use the car.

Tom was beyond excited at the way God answered this prayer. When the family left their country to come home, they had no car. When they landed, Tom was able to give them the good news that they would be getting our car.

You cannot make this kind of stuff up! It is events like this in my life that strengthen my faith and let me know there is a God in the universe who listens and answers prayers. What a blessing for our family to be the answer to that prayer request.

When we were in Houston Texas, I had lost my company car when I took a HQ job and had to buy a car to get back and forth to work.

We had been there about 18 months when one Sunday morning we read in the church bulletin that there was a need for a good used car. My Bride leaned over and told me that I was going to get promoted and moved back to Atlanta and get a new company car, so we could donate our car to the church.

I laughed, because I was not looking for a new job, there were not any prospects on the horizon and that just seemed ridiculous.

Two weeks later I got a promotion, a new company car and we donated that car to the church! Gods timing is always so good. As you will see in the next chapter, my Bride knew something I did not. She had been praying to move back home.

Tools

This summer my family and I went on a short-term mission trip to a Word of Life camp in Cochabamba Bolivia. We had been praying about where God would lead us to serve this year, and we were very excited when the door opened for us to go to Bolivia.

As we prepared for our trip I sent a note to the team leader and asked him what sorts of things we could bring to bless the missionaries at the camp.

He sent a long note and list of possible things – soap, food, clothing, books, etc. etc.   The one interesting thing he suggested was to bring tools. Now if you have ever traveled internationally, you know you only get a certain number of bags and a certain weight limit and tools are very heavy. Therefore I had completely discounted the thought of taking tools.

However, as we got closer to the time to leave, I could not get tools off of my heart and mind. It was like that itch on your back that you cannot scratch and will not go away.   Since four of us were going, we could take 8 bags with us and as I weighted each bag, it was obvious we would have room and weight limit to take some tools.

Therefore I went to the local hardware store and loaded up with all kinds of hand tools - hammers, pliers, screwdrivers, levels, measuring tapes etc. etc. I also got a tool bag to put them in and organize them.

 To my surprise when we got there, the camp had an entire workshop with more tools than I had at home – and that is saying something because I love woodworking. I was puzzled by the need for tools and let it linger in the back of my mind.

As each day went by, we would have lunch and dinner with different groups of missionaries and it was a blessed time to hear them share their stories and their needs.

On the last night, we broke into groups of men and women and had a separate time of Bible study and sharing. As the women left to go to another room, the men began sharing. The missionaries all shared their stories of how they came to be Christians, their family and then their calling to ministry. The spoke about their needs and challenges as well as opportunities.

When they had all finished, our leader asked them if there was anything we could pray for and or anything we could do for them. He specifically called out their financial needs and asked them to expound upon that.

Two of the men (Alberto and Puma) stated that they had little to no financial support, but were trusting the Lord to supply their needs. They did say that they were carpenters, but were in need of hand tools as well as power tools. If they could have these tools, then it would empower them to be "tent makers" like the Apostle Paul and supply their own support by working as they were doing ministry.

At the moment, I knew why I had brought the bag of tools. It was for these two gentleman to use in their ministry.

After we had finished that evening, I pulled them aside and asked them to come to my room. I presented them with the gift of the tools and tool bag, and they were happy beyond belief. They thanked me repeatedly and gave praise and honor to God; as did I! It was God who had worked all of this out in His perfect and wonderful timing. We were so blessed to be an answer to these missionaries prayers and blessed to see how God worked it all out.

Answered Prayer

The following are all true stories from our own life and experience. I hope as you read these you will see how God can work and move in the believer's life. As I have said several times in this book, God is a good, good father!

Moving Back

I have been working for Coca-Cola for 20+ years now. In that time I have seen many ups and downs with the company.

When I first started out with the company it was with a division called "Coca-Cola Foods" which was later to be called "The Minute Maid Company". My original job was in Atlanta which is the hometown for both Coca-Cola and for my Bride (where we met and married).

Unfortunately, 4 months into my career with Coca-Cola, they restructured the company and I was offered a promotion and new job in Houston – which was the headquarters of Coca-Cola foods. Being, young and dumb, I took my Bride and two young children to Texas for our next great adventure.

To make a long story shorter, the job was tough and challenging, the climate hot but not unbearable, and the people very friendly and sociable. But in the end it was not "home". My Bride especially was homesick.

One of the things we had decided early in our marriage was how we would spend the Thanksgiving and Christmas holidays. We decided for Thanksgiving if we were living away from Atlanta, we would travel home to be visit with our families and we would always stay home for Christmas and create our own family memories.

So that year we loaded up the kids and made the 17 hour drive from Houston to Atlanta. I knew we were in trouble when it took us 5 hours just to get out of Texas.

It was good to get home and the kids (we only had two of our four at that point – Hannah and David) we very excited to spend time with their grandparents. Debbie's mom was the kids favorites and she loved on them and doted on them just as you would expect a good grandmother to do. The kids even had a special name for her. They called her "Mongee", it was a made up name that Hannah came up with as a little girl and it stuck. She loved being Mongee. She was the only one!

When we got back to Houston after the holidays, it was very stressful and Debbie and I one of our bigger fights about jobs, moving and where "home" really was. Needless to say, I was the bad guy who was pretty insensitive to my Bride's feelings and her heart's desire. So unbeknownst to me, my Bride and daughter started praying for a move back home to Atlanta.

That year for Christmas, Hannah had wanted a bicycle very badly and she started praying for her bike. However, one day as she was praying with my Bride, she asked why couldn't we move back and be closer to Mongee.

So she and my Bride started praying for a new job for me that would move us back to Atlanta.

In the previous chapter you read about how one day at church there was a notice that said they were looking for someone to donate a good used car. My Bride leaned over and told me we were going to be the ones who donated the car because I was going to get promoted and we were moving back to Atlanta.

I laughed and told her it was ridiculous. There were no jobs in Atlanta and it would take a miracle from God for a job to be created.

The very next day at work, I received a call from a friend of mine in Atlanta who told me they were creating a brand new job in Atlanta and I would be perfect for the role. I was floored!

I immediately called home and told my Bride, " you are not going to believe what just happened". She was so happy and thrilled and we all praised God and were amazed at His timing and goodness.

God knew the desires of my daughter's heart and the desires of my Brides heart and He was opening a door for our family to move back home to Atlanta.

Needless to say, I interviewed for the job and got it!

Along with the new job came a promotion, and a company car. We promptly donated our car to the church and packed up to move back to Atlanta.

With God, it is all about the timing and how He builds our faith and trust over the days, weeks and years thorough His faithfulness and love. Does he always give us what we want when we want it? No, of course not. He gives us what we need, when we need it.

He is our good, good Father.

The Room Key

It is really appropriate that I am writing this chapter this afternoon while I am sitting in a rented condo at the beach. We have just started our annual family vacation and reading and writing are two of the most relaxing things that I do while we are at the beach.

This answered prayer took place about 20 years ago when we were staying at a different condo farther down the beach.

We decided as a family many years ago that vacation time was an investment in our time together to rest, relax, and recharge our batteries. I carve out time from work and make sure to completely unplug from the grid. I literally turn off my work cell phone and work computer and store them in a cabinet at home for the duration of our vacation. That way, it is impossible for anyone from work to reach me (I sell water with bubble and water without bubbles – so we don't have any real emergencies).

Anyway, on this particular vacation, it was late in the evening and very dark outside (no moon). The kids wanted to take some flashlights and go out on the beach and look for crabs and other sea creatures that may be roaming about.

It is always a blast, so out the door we go with four flashlights (we only had Hannah and David at that time and they were 7 and 5 years old). Soon the kids were running here and there and my Bride and I are doing our best to herd the cats.

After a while we all grew weary and decided to head back inside. As we started back to the condo, I reached into my pocket for the room key and realized it was not there. In a panic, we started sweeping the beach for the key. We looked for about 10 minutes and realized the futility of finding a small key in a vast ocean of sand.

These were the days before cell phones were common, so I really did not know what we were going to do. I could not get in the car – the keys were in the condo and we did not know anybody in the condo complex (we just rented a place there).

So I just stopped the family right there and told them we were going to pray and ask God to help us find the room key. We gathered in a little circle to pray.

I don't know why, but we turned off all of our flashlights and I offered up a prayer to God about helping us find the key. In their child like faith, my children also asked God to help us find the key as well. We said Amen and then turned our flashlights back on.

I shone my light on the sand by my feet and God as my witness, there was the key! We all shouted for joy and praised God! It was unbelievable. I know this sounds like a story too good to be true, but it's not. God is so good all the time and I often think of this story and God's concern for a panicked father who did not know what he was going to do that night without intervention from his heavenly father.

The Bolivian Connection

One of my goals as a father is to introduce my children to God and His working around the world through missions and missionaries. So we set the goal of having our children be on each of the 6 continents (not including Antarctica) before they graduate from high school. We did not get a chance to do this with our two oldest (Hannah and David), but we are well on our way with Sarah Grace and Jonathan.

So far, Sarah Grace has been on mission's trips to:

North America
Africa
Europe
South American

We hope in 2018 to be in Asia and in 2019 to be in Australia (Lord willing).

This year we planned to go to South America and prayed about the doors God would open for us on that continent. Originally, we had planned to go to Ecuador (where I had been before), but ultimately we ended up in Bolivia.

It was an amazing trip and God is doing a great work through Word of Life in Cochabamba.

Each evening, we had dinner with a different group of missionaries working in the camp and it was such a blessing to hear their stories of God's faithfulness.

We heard time and again each evening how the missionaries did not have 100% of their support raised, but how God ALWAYS met their need and answered their prayer just when they needed provision.

One story really touched my heart and showed how God is concerned with the simplest needs, wants and desires in our life.

One of the missionary ladies had been praying about dish towels! Yes dish towels. Certainly, not something that would even start to cross our minds in the richness of America. We would just go to Target or Wal-Mart or wherever and just buy the dish towels and be done with it.

That does not work in Bolivia, when you do not even have the resources to purchase the dish towels. In this instance, she started praying that God would provide dish towels; it was a simple, honest plea for a common need.

When a new group of folks on a short-term mission trip came to the camp, they were working and helping as usual. One day, the ladies in the group decided to go to the market and buy groceries to bless the missionaries in the camp. While they were at the store, one of the ladies decided to throw in some dish towels along with the food. She did not know about the need or prayer request from the missionary family.

You can imagine the tears of surprise and gratitude when the family received this gift.

They told us story, upon story like this where God was faithful to meet their need and answer their prayers. It was awe-inspiring to see how they lived their life by trust and faith in God.

It is so cool to see how God continues to work and answer prayers!

Seats on a Plane

My youngest daughter is Sarah Grace and she just turned 16 years old and has a beautiful voice and loves to sing and performs in musicals and choir.

I had a huge surprise for Sarah Grace when she turned 16!

Here in Atlanta the Broadway shows come to town and Sarah Graces' favorite musical is Phantom of The Opera. It came to town in March which is the also the month she was born.

So what I did was tell her I had purchased tickets to Phantom of the Opera for her birthday and I was going take her to see it at the Fox Theater in Atlanta. But the surprise was this, I actually took her to NYC to see the "real" Phantom of The Opera on Broadway.

It was a day trip! We got up at 3:30 in the morning because our flight to NYC was at 6:30 am. I had purchased the plane tickets months in advance and because of new airline rules (and the cheap seats), I could not confirm our actual seats until 24 hours before the trip. For the trip up to NYC I was able to snag two seats together but unfortunately, for the trip home we would be widely separated and the flight was completely sold out.

I knew Sarah Grace would be very nervous and anxious about having to sit by herself, next to some stranger. I started praying about the seat and did not mention anything to Sarah Grace. There was no reason to worry her unnecessarily.

Our flight up was uneventful and we had a blast! We went to the Empire State Building, rode the subway, went to see the Statue of Liberty, had some good pizza, saw the show, went to central park and wandered around Manhattan. It was a great and glorious day with my young daughter. However in the back of my mind I was thinking about and praying about the seat on the plane.

When we got to the airport that evening I finally told her about the seating situation and that I had been praying about it. If necessary, I would pay someone else for their seat (nobody would want my seat voluntarily – it was a middle seat in the back of the plane).

As we waited to board, they asked for volunteers to give up their seats because the plane was overbooked. This did not look good for us.

We finally boarded the plane and Sarah took her seat and I went back to my seat. The plane was one of those with two seats on the left and three seats on the right.

I could see Sarah up ahead of me, she was sitting next to the window and the aisle seat next to her was empty.

The plane slowly filled up and I watch all manner of humanity walk onto the plane and I wondered who would be the person to sit next to my daughter? Could they be persuaded to give up their seat and switch with me? How much would it cost me? What if they said "NO"! I continued to pray.

I know this seems like a silly thing to pray about, but it was important to me to finish the day well. I was making a dream come true for my daughter and I did not want it potentially ruined at the very end of the day. It was the desire of my heart to sit next to my daughter.

As the flood of people became a trickle, the seat next to her was still empty. My guess is now they would start to call all the standby passengers and the seat would soon be taken. Time seemed to slow down as I held my breath and waited for that final person to walk down the aisle and take the seat.

Then to my surprise the flight attendant told us the forward boarding door had been closed and we were preparing to take off. I called the flight attendant closest to me and explained my situation and asked if I could go and sit next to my daughter and of course she said yes (although she did tell me to make it snappy).

Needless to say, this father was VERY happy and so was his daughter. We had a wonderful flight home and the memory was complete.

Now some of you will read this and call it luck or chance. That is certainly a world view that some may have, but I believe in the power of prayer and know that my God is concerned even with the little aspects of our life.

Could He have chosen for that seat to be taken? Yes it could have happened, and he would still be God and I could and would still praise Him, but He chose to hear a father's simple prayer and answer it.

I choose to believe!

The Hurricane Surprise

This past Christmas, my mother-in-law reminded me of an amazing story of answered prayer and God's faithfulness in the midst of a crisis.

My father-in-law had been in poor health for many years and was really starting to decline very quickly. He was at the point of needing oxygen 24/7. It was literally a matter of life & death if he did not have his oxygen.

Luckily, there are portable oxygen machines that allowed him to have some flexibility and travel. He loved the beach and ocean so very much and even if he could not go onto the sand and into the water, he just wanted to be near enough to see and experience the moment.

He and my mother-in-law decided to drive down to Florida and take some much needed time away as he health was slipping further. They checked the weather (as it was hurricane season), and the only hurricane threat was far from where they were planning to vacation, so off they went.

It took a couple of days to drive to their destination, and in that time the hurricane had strengthened and changed paths. Luckily for them, they had enough time to change their path as well and give the hurricane a wide berth..... or so they thought.

They headed to Long Boat Key to find a hotel and try to salvage some of their vacation time. Unfortunately, all of the hotels were booked with people fleeing the hurricane. As they drove along they pulled into a very small motel parking lot and thought they would ask if there was any availability. As they got out of their van, a couple was exiting the motel and asked if they were looking for a room. My in-laws were very excited about the prospect of finding a place to stay and indicated the needed a room. They immediately booked the ground floor room and checked into the motel.

The hurricane quickly changes its path and headed towards them. It was too late to evacuate as the bridge to the mainland was closed, so they were forced to hunker down and weather the storm. Their biggest fear was losing electricity, because the oxygen concentrator needed constant power to work.

The manager of the hotel came by and warned everyone that most likely they would be losing power and it would be off for several days. If that happened, my father-in-law would surely die.

As the storm drew near, they stopped and prayed that the electricity would not go out and the building would keep them safe. My mother-in-law then went for a quick walk outside while she still had the chance and was continuing to pray for the electricity and their safety.

As she turned to go back to her room, she saw a rainbow just above their little motel and she just knew everything was going to be alright.

When the storm hit, the power across the street went out. Then the buildings to their left lost power and a short time later the buildings to the right lost power. They were literally the only place with power as far as the eye could see. They were the lighthouse in the middle of this terrible storm.

Several days passed before the streets were cleared and the bridge was opened and they could leave the island. In that span of time, the power in their little motel never went out. There were no backup generators and no other way to account for the power staying on other than the power of prayer.

God is good all the time! Even in the midst of a terrible tempest.

Visa

As a family, we have been going on mission trips around the world for a number of years. We want to intentionally expose our children the God's Kingdom work around the world and see people praying, praising, and worshiping God in their own language and culture. It is so incredibly powerful to worship with other believers, even if you cannot understand their language.

It is a wonderful opportunity and we praise God that we have been able to travel extensively to see God working all over the world.

On one of our trips, we were going to need a Visa to enter the country, so each of us applied for a Visa and in fairly short order we had approval for three of the four Visa's we would need. However, there was a delay with Jonathan's Visa and we were concerned. If we could not secure his Visa, we would have to cancel the trip (we were not going without him).

At the same time, as we were preparing for the trip, we had several people drop out of the team and our mission partners were worried that perhaps God was closing the door and we might want to reconsider making the trip. They sent me a message to this effect and we agreed to pray and ask God to clearly show us His will and way for this trip.

I remember it was 6:00 in the morning and I was sitting in my car in the parking garage at work and concerned about the direction of this team I was leading. I immediately called my Bride and updated her on the situation. I asked her if she had any trepidation or concern in her heart and mind about the trip. I wanted to make sure we were still aligned on the project.

She agreed that we were aligned and felt God was calling us to go. We prayed over the phone for some time and just asked God to clearly speak to us and show us how to proceed.

When I hung up the phone with my Bride, I decided to look at my e-mail on my phone before I went to start my exercise in the company gym. I had checked all of my e-mail before I left the house at 4:30 am to make sure there were no "burning bridges" overnight, but before I started a two hour workout, I just wanted one more quick peak.

To my surprise there was one e-mail that had just arrived! It was from the Embassy and it was a confirmation that Jonathan's Visa had just been approved!! Wow, talk about amazing timing. In the next instant, I received a message from our mission partner who said we should proceed with our original plans and finish the preparation for the trip.

Was this luck, chance or serendipity? Of course not! It was the power and majesty of our great Lord and Savior who answered a prayer at just the right time to increase our faith and belief. Skeptics will say "well you would have gotten the Visa approval no matter what – the timing is just coincidental". And that is the difference between those of us who believe there is a God who chooses to answer prayer and those who believe they are the masters of their own universe. I believe! What about you?

The Parking Space

Time away alone with my Bride is an important investment in our marriage and relationship. We learned long ago that if we were not careful to make these time investments in our relationship, it would start to suffer and we would all be miserable.

In the winter we like to rent a small cabin between Christmas and New Years and spend the time relaxing and reflecting on the past year. We have been doing this for a long time and it has always been very helpful.

However, we had never taken time away together in the beginning of the year. If had been a cold winter, so a warm destination seems appropriate.

Valentine's day was going to be on a Monday, so I decided to whisk my Bride away to Miami for a long weekend and valentines celebration.

We just wanted to chill out for most of the time, and the only real plans we had for that weekend was a daytrip to Key West. It was about a 3 hour drive from Miami and would be a fun adventure.

When we got Miami, we took Uber to our hotel and when we got there, we noticed there was no parking at all. I had planned to rent a car the next day and needed to know where to park. I asked the front desk and they told me they only had valet parking and it would be $45 per day. Wow, my car rental was only going to cost $30. I had not planned on this.

So I asked if there was public parking and the closest place was over a mile away and $25 per day. I could try to find a place on the street, but parking was limited to 3 hours at time, and we did not see any parking spaces open.....ever!

Anyway, the next day we rented the car and headed off to Key West. It was a long and beautiful drive and we had so much fun that day. We stayed until sunset and enjoyed the warm weather and festive atmosphere.

Before we started to drive back, my Bride and I stopped and prayed about a parking space. We asked God to provide one close to the hotel as it would be very late when we would get home and I was not anxious to valet park or public part a mile away.

It was a wonderful evening and a great ride home. I love spending time with my beautiful Bride!

As we got closer to the hotel, we noticed there were no open parking spots! NONE. It was very disconcerting. It was almost mid-night and we were both tired.

I decided to drop my Bride off at the hotel and the go in search of a parking space. As I dropped her off at the front door, I decided to circle the block and see if there might be a parking space.

And guess what.....
That's right, I found a parking space just around the corner from the hotel. The rest of the street was full of cars, but there was this one beautiful parking spot.

But wait, it gets better.

Because it was just after mid-night, I only had to pay a dollar to park from mid-night to 3:00 am and then it was FREE parking until 9:00 am the next morning.

Not only did God provide a perfect parking space, He also made it unbelievably affordable. He really is a good, good father.

Based on my study of prayer, there is nothing to small or insignificant we can ask of God. I choose to believe He opened up a parking space for me and my Bride. Now clearly this is not nearly as miraculous as the parting of the Red Sea, healing someone from cancer nor sparing someone from disaster. But my God is a good, good father and I know my Father in heaven hears even the smallest of prayers. I choose to give God all the honor and glory and praise and to continually be thankful for all His blessing large and small in my life.

What do you believe? Some may judge me for including what they consider a trivial and mundane prayer request. However, I would submit to you that our lives are filled with many more ordinary and mundane tasks than with disasters and trials. Seek today to trust God in all things. He has so much more to show us each and every day.

Seek Him out this week in the ordinary and mundane and see how He chooses to answer you. You might just be surprised

Continual Prayer

While I have shared with you some very specific prayer requests that were for immediate needs, I also wanted to share with you my ongoing and or continual prayer requests. These are from my prayer journal and I have them broken up into several categories.

These are all part of my daily prayers.

Personal

After having asked God to forgive me for any specific transgression, these are all prayers and requests for myself as I start each day.

"You have put me in this world for something Lord, show me what it is and help me to work out the purpose in my life"

"What will you do through me today?"

These are two very intentional and purposeful prayer requests. It is a reminder to constantly be on the lookout for God's leading in my life. Sometimes it will be through my prayer, mediation and study time, sometimes it will through circumstances and at other times it will be through individuals. No matter the source, God can speak into my life if I am actively looking and listening.

If I am looking for God to show me my purpose in life (long term), as well as a clear focus on opportunities immediately before me (short term), then hopefully I can stay grounded in my walk and have a positive testimony and influence on others.

I then have some very specific things that I pray about each and every time:

- Wisdom
- Discernment
- Keep me close and clean
- Right attitude
- Contentment, but not resignation
- Hedge of protection (guard my eyes, ears, tongue, heart and mind)
- Pray that I will be the best husband, father, friend, employee I need to be
- That I would be intentional
- That I would finish well
- Fruits of the spirit to be evident in my life (love, joy, peace, patience, kindness, goodness, faithfulness, gentleness and self-control)
- Opportunities to teach and share
- That I would be a dream maker and not a dream taker
- That I would be generous giver
- That I would be an encourager
- Opportunities for mentorship
- Specific mission trips (in this case right now I am preparing for trips to Bolivia and Vietnam)

Prayers for my Bride

After praying for myself, I then prioritize my prayers for my Bride:

- For our relationship
- Blessing upon her
- Wisdom
- Discernment
- Finish well
- Give her the desires of her heart
- Right attitude
- Hedge of protection (guard her eyes, ears, tongue, heart and mind)
- Fruits of the spirit to be evident in her life (love, joy, peace, patience, kindness, goodness, faithfulness, gentleness and self-control)

Prayers for my Children

After praying for Bride, I then prioritize my prayers for my children:

- For our relationship
- I pray for their future spouse and for the parents of their future spouse. I have been praying for Hannah's husband for 25 years!
- Blessing upon each of them
- Bring people of positive influence into their life (this is especially important for my kids who are grown and live away)
- Wisdom
- Discernment
- Finish well
- Right attitude
- Keep them close and clean
- Hedge of protection (guard her eyes, ears, tongue, heart and mind)
- Fruits of the spirit to be evident in her life (love, joy, peace, patience, kindness, goodness, faithfulness, gentleness and self-control)

Prayers for Others

After praying for family, I then offer up prayers for the following:

- Immediate family (parents, siblings, cousins etc.)
- Pastor of our church
- Close friends
- Work associates
- People I am mentoring
- Missionaries we are supporting
- Other specific prayer requests

I am a big believer in continually praying for wisdom and discernment. True wisdom only comes from God and like Solomon if I can have only one thing, it would be a wise and discerning heart and mind.

Proverbs 2:6-8

For the Lord gives wisdom;
From His mouth come knowledge and understanding.

James 1:5-8

But if any of you lacks wisdom, let him ask of God, who gives to all generously and without reproach, and it will be given to him.

Proverbs 3:13

How blessed is the man who finds wisdom
And the man who gains understanding.

Think about it, what situation in your life could not be better if you had more wisdom and discernment.   Wisdom and discernment permeate all aspects of your physical, mental and spiritual being.

These are my daily thoughts and prayers that I am continually offering up to God.   We are taught in the Bible to "pray without ceasing" and that the "effective and fervent prayer of a righteous man can accomplish much".

Therefore, God not only expects, but desires for us to bring our prayers and petitions to him all the time.

1 Thessalonians 5:16-18

*Rejoice always; **pray without ceasing**; in everything give thanks; for this is God's will for you in Christ Jesus.*

Ephesians 6:18

With all prayer and petition pray at all times in the Spirit, and with this in view, be on the alert with all perseverance and petition for all the saints,

James 5:16

Therefore, confess your sins to one another, and pray for one another so that you may be healed. The effective prayer of a righteous man can accomplish much.

Finally, in the parable below, Jesus is teaching us about being persistent and continual in our prayer. We are constantly supposed to bring our prayers to the Lord; he is willing and waiting to hear our prayers and petitions.

<u>Luke 18:1-8</u>

Now He was telling them a parable to show that **at all times they ought to pray and not to lose heart,** *saying, "In a certain city there was a judge who did not fear God and did not respect man. There was a widow in that city, and she kept coming to him, saying, 'Give me legal protection from my opponent.' For a while he was unwilling; but afterward he said to himself, 'Even though I do not fear God nor respect man, yet because this widow bothers me, I will give her legal protection, otherwise by continually coming she will wear me out.'" And the Lord said, "Hear what the unrighteous judge said; now, will not God bring about justice for His elect who cry to Him day and night, and will He delay long over them? I tell you that He will bring about justice for them quickly. However, when the Son of Man comes, will He find faith on the earth?"*

There is a young man I have known for many years who once had a close walk with the Lord. I ran into his parents several years ago and inquired as to his well-being. They were heartbroken to tell me he had proclaimed himself an atheist and had walked away from the faith. These were two Godly people (he was a preacher) and it very sad to hear this report. I added this young man to my prayer list and will keep him there with the hope of his retuning to the faith. This is a marathon and not a sprint and we should continually be praying for those who are on the long road of life.

Why Pray

The best place to look for answers on prayer and the best commentary on prayer is the Bible itself.

The short answer on "why pray" is because it is effective and this is the way we communicate our wants, needs and desires to God.   The Bible tells us in the book of James that the effective prayer of a righteous man can accomplish much.

I actually like how James 5:16 is rendered in different Bible translations:

James 5:16

...The effective prayer of a righteous man can accomplish much.

Depending on the translation, the verse says that prayer:

- Is Powerful
- Is Effective
- Has a mighty influence
- Can accomplish much

No matter the translation, it is clear that the intent of James was to convey to the reader that your prayers have an influence on God and that we must be persistent and bring our prayers and petitions to Him.

Here is what you will see as we study some different verses from the Bible:

- **God is listening! He hears us!**

- **If you are suffering you should pray**

- **Call upon God when you are in trouble**

- **God will answer us when we pray**

- **God is with us all the time**

- **God wants to rescue us and save us**

- **God is with you in the storm**

Now, let's examine the different Bible verses that compel us to pray.

We will start with the book of James (a powerful and incredibly insightful book of the Bible) and then follow the path of scripture as it leads us through the reasons to pray.

James 5:13

Is anyone among you suffering? Then he must pray.

This is a great start! Sometimes the easy answer is not the one we want to hear or try. We are designed for the complicated. We want some sort of high tech solution or 15 step plan. James keeps it simple - If you are suffering, pray to God!

Psalm 50:15

Call upon Me in the day of trouble;
I shall rescue you, and you will honor Me."

Psalm 91:15

"He will call upon Me, and I will answer him;
I will be with him in trouble;
I will rescue him and honor him.

Psalm 107:6

Then they cried out to the Lord in their trouble;
He delivered them out of their distresses.

Psalm 107:13

Then they cried out to the Lord in their trouble;
He saved them out of their distresses.

Psalm 81:7

"You called in trouble and I rescued you;
I answered you in the hiding place of thunder;
I proved you at the waters of Meribah.   Selah.

God is listening and wants us to bring our prayers and petitions to him. He is a good father who stands ready to rescue his children.   Note in the previous verses that not only did God deliver them, but He also talks about being there with them in the trouble as well. Sometimes the answer does not come right away, but know that God is in your midst even in the middle of the storm.

Matthew 7:7

"Ask, and it will be given to you; seek, and you will find; knock, and it will be opened to you.

Matthew 21:22

And all things you ask in prayer, believing, you will receive."

Psalm 107:28-30

Then they cried to the Lord in their trouble,
And He brought them out of their distresses.
He caused the storm to be still,
So that the waves of the sea were hushed.
Then they were glad because they were quiet,
So He guided them to their desired haven.

Mark 11:24

Therefore I say to you, all things for which you pray and ask, believe that you have received them, and they will be granted you.

John 14:13-14

Whatever you ask in My name, that will I do, so that the Father may be glorified in the Son. If you ask Me anything in My name, I will do it.

Psalm 116:1-2

I love the Lord, because He hears
My voice and my supplications.
Because He has inclined His ear to me,
Therefore I shall call upon Him as long as I live.

Philippians 4:6

Be anxious for nothing, but in everything by prayer and supplication with thanksgiving let your requests be made known to God.

Wow – easier said than done.   How often do we worry and fret over things that have not even happened yet.   I have heard it said that 90% of the things we worry about never come to pass.

So, from all of these verses, what can we determine about prayer?

- **God is listening! He hears us!**

- **If you are suffering you should pray**

- **Call upon God when you are in trouble**

- **God will answer us when we pray**

- **God is with us all the time**

- **God wants to rescue us and save us**

- **God is with you**

I think it is important to interject here that an answer to prayer can be NO! We tend to only think in terms of God saying YES to our prayers but we must remember that only HE can see end to end and there will be times when the answer to our prayers will be no.   It is at this point that we have to have the spiritual maturity to understand that there may still be things for us to learn from the troubles we are in.   God desire is to draw near to us and have us draw near to him.

Now, Let us first examine some of the different Bible characters and see what we can learn about prayer in times of difficulty and adversity.

Elijah

In 1 Kings Chapter 17 & 18, we find the story of Elijah and his need for an answered prayer in his time of trouble and turmoil.

Elijah is an interesting character. He comes on the scene at a time when there were wicked kings leading that nation of Israel. He has a tough task as God is going to have Elijah confront the king and others.

After facing King Ahab the first time and telling him there would be no rain until he spoke again, God called him away.   First he went to a small brook and the ravens brought him food.   Eventually the brook dried up and then God told him to go to a widow's home.

It is here we see his first answered prayer after the son of the widow dies. He takes the son upstairs and asks God to restore his life

1 Kings 17:21-22

Then he stretched himself upon the child three times, and called to the Lord and said, "O Lord my God, I pray You, let this child's life return to him." The Lord heard the voice of Elijah, and the life of the child returned to him and he revived.

God is gracious and answers the prayer. In doing so the widows faith is increased and she knows a real man of God has been in her home.

Elijah then returns to confront King Ahab.

How would you like to be surrounded by 850 people who did not like you? And oh by the way the King and Queen don't really care for you either!

Don't you think that perhaps praying to God would be a good thing?

Elijah was definitely not liked or appreciated by King Ahab. Elijah was the chosen prophet of the time and he had said to King Ahab that there would be no more rain until he spoke again. Several years pass, and then Elijah goes back before King Ahab and the King is less than pleased to see him.

He calls him a "troubler, troublemaker, or destroyer of Israel". You can only imagine that this is not a good place to be in terms of your relationship with the King. The King literally had the power of life and death in his hands and being on his bad side would not bode well for you!

Elijah then goes on to challenge King Ahab and the prophets of Baal. He basically threw down the gauntlet and told the King to bring the 450 prophets of Baal and the 400 prophets of Asherah to Mount Carmel and see who served the real God.

This was life and death! If God does not answer his prayer, he will be toast!

The challenge is simple in that each group would ask God to answer with fire from heaven to take up their sacrifice.

After the prophets of Baal had failed (Elijah actually taunted and mocked them, it is really quite funny), it was Elijah's turn and this was his prayer:

1 Kings 18:36-37

At the time of the offering of the evening sacrifice, Elijah the prophet came near and said, "O Lord, the God of Abraham, Isaac and Israel, today let it be known that You are God in Israel and that I am Your servant and I have done all these things at Your word. Answer me, O Lord, answer me, that this people may know that You, O Lord, are God, and that You have turned their heart back again."

The good news is that God did answer his prayers and delivered him an incredible miracle in the face of his enemies. Read the story for yourself and be inspired by the prayer of this man of God.

Jehoshaphat

In 2 Chronicles chapter 20, we find the story of Jehoshaphat

Jehoshaphat is now King of Israel and he is suddenly faced with a huge problem.   Several of his enemies have combined forces and they are going to attack.   This is a life and death situation where thousands could be slaughtered.   So what does Jehoshaphat decide to do?

He chooses to pray!

He acknowledges the following in his prayer to God: (verses 6-12)
- God is sovereign
- He is THE GOD
- God has the power to answer prayer
- Reminds God of His promises
- Accepts the fact they are powerless in the face of the enemy
- He does not know what to do!

In verse 12 we see how he concludes his prayer

2 Chronicles 20:12

O our God, will You not judge them? For we are powerless before this great multitude who are coming against us; nor do we know what to do, but our eyes are on You."

Jehoshaphat knows he cannot defeat the enemy without God's assistance.

Again, God answers the prayer in a very cool way! He speaks through one of the Levites named Jahaziel and tells them the following:

- The battle belongs to God
- Do not fear
- The Lord is with them

The enemies are defeated and the people of Israel did not even have to fight. God made the enemies turn on themselves and destroy each other. All the people of Israel did was sing praises and give thanks to God as this unfolded before their very eyes.

I think the three things listed here really encapsulate our relationship with God.

- He is with us,
- He does not want us to fear
- He stands ready to fight the battles for us.

He really is a good father. What good father does not want to do all of those things for his children?

Jabez

Not much is known about Jabez other than he was an honorable man and his mother gave him a unique name. He is only mentioned twice in the entire Bible and yet he offers a powerful prayer that God answers.

Jabez may have been an obscure character in the Bible, but it is no accident that he was included in God's holy word. It is clear Jabez knew the God he was praying to was "THE GOD" of Israel. He prayed with confidence and asked for God's blessing as well as God's protection. He was looking for God's leading and direction as he asked that God's hand would be with him. He knew if he was blessed, he would need the guiding hand of God to allow him to use the blessing in a way pleasing to God.

We may not know much about Jabez, but we do know a lot about God and his goodness, mercy, grace, faithfulness and love. He is a good father who only wants the best for his children. Sometimes, we just have to ask.

1 Chronicles 4:9-10

Jabez was more honorable than his brothers, and his mother named him Jabez saying, "Because I bore him with pain." Now Jabez called on the God of Israel, saying, "Oh that You would bless me indeed and enlarge my border, and that Your hand might be with me, and that You would keep me from harm that it may not pain me!" And God granted him what he requested.

Jonah

Many of you know the story of Jonah. He was called by God to go preach to the people of Nineveh. Instead, he tries to flee from God (which is quite funny to think that there is any place we could actually hide from God) by taking a ship the farthest point from and in the opposite direction of Nineveh.

God had other plans for him. As the ship is tossed about in a storm, his fellow passengers realize he is the reason for all of their troubles. They heave him overboard to calm the tempest.

Jonah was swallowed by a great fish and was in the belly for three days and nights. While he was in the stomach of the fish, he offered up prayers to God. As you can imagine, this would be a good time to pray! In Jonah chapter 2 you can read how he cried out to God and praised Him even in the midst of his unique situation.

Jonah 2:1-2

Then Jonah prayed to the Lord his God from the stomach of the fish, and he said,

> *"I called out of my distress to the Lord,*
> *And He answered me.*
> *I cried for help from the depth of Sheol;*
> *You heard my voice.*

Few of us will ever be in a predicament as challenging as Jonah, but it is clear that he was in a place where he could do nothing for himself. He was literally stuck until God was ready to deliver him. He did the one thing that he knew he could do and that was to pray.

Is prayer your "go to" answer when you are in trouble? Do you seek God's face when storms and trials present themselves? How much are you trying to do in your own power and strength? Jonah thought he had all the answers and thought he could run away. You can never run so far or so fast that God will not already be there with you. Instead of running from God, run to God and see for yourself the plans He has for you.

David

David is a character who was constantly praying to God as he faced trials and tribulations in his life (many of these trials were from men trying to kill him)

- Goliath
- Saul
- Absalom (his son)

You can read the many different Psalms that David wrote when he was in trouble. David was constantly crying out to God. Remember that David was a man after God's own heart and he prayed with the hope and knowledge that God was listening and would answer his cries and petitions. We can learn a lot by reading the psalms about how to pray and reach out to God and the example that David gave us.

Here are some examples of David crying out to God:

Psalm 3:4

I was crying to the Lord with my voice,
And He answered me from His holy mountain. Selah.

Psalm 4:1

.
Answer me when I call, O God of my righteousness!
You have relieved me in my distress;
Be gracious to me and hear my prayer.

Psalm 57:1

Be gracious to me, O God, be gracious to me,
For my soul takes refuge in You;
And in the shadow of Your wings I will take refuge
Until destruction passes by.

Take the time read and study the Psalms. They are a source of great encouragement and solace when you are in the storms of life.

Nehemiah

Nehemiah is an amazing and often overlooked character in the Bible. He was the cupbearer to King Artaxerxes while in captivity in Babylon. He had heard about the destruction of the walls and gates of Jerusalem and this greatly discouraged him.

He immediately offered a prayer to God such that he could return and rebuild the city of Jerusalem. What follows is God answering his prayers through the king.

What I find most interesting is the numerous times Nehemiah stops in the middle of discussions and prays! He was a man who knew that prayer was something that is done anywhere at any time.

Nehemiah was in the middle of a discussion with the King and he stopped and prayed right then:

Nehemiah 2:4-5

Then the king said to me, "What would you request?" **So I prayed to the God of heaven**. *I said to the king, "If it please the king, and if your servant has found favor before you, send me to Judah, to the city of my fathers' tombs, that I may rebuild it."*

Next in chapter 4, we find several of the men ridiculing the work that Nehemiah was doing to restore the wall. We pick up the conversation where Nehemiah calls out to God in the midst of this ridicule:

Nehemiah 4:3-5

Now Tobiah the Ammonite was near him and he said, "Even what they are building – if a fox should jump on it, he would break their stone wall down!"

Hear, O our God, how we are despised! Return their reproach on their own heads and give them up for plunder in a land of captivity. Do not forgive their iniquity and let not their sin be blotted out before You, for they have demoralized the builders.

Nehemiah knew the right time to call out to God was right then and there! He was trusting God to be their provider and protector. He was also setting an example to others working on the wall as he prayed. He wanted them to know (as well as his enemies), that God was for them!

In chapter 6 we find the enemies of Nehemiah plotting to harm him so as to prevent the rebuilding of the walls and gates. They sent letters to frighten him, they sent messengers of gloom and doom, they condemned him and made false reports against him. As all of this is going on, Nehemiah asks God to be his defender:

Nehemiah 6:14

Remember, O my God, Tobiah and Sanballat according to these works of theirs, and also Noadiah the prophetess and the rest of the prophets who were trying to frighten me.

Nehemiah was a man who knew to pray and reach out to God in the moment. He did not wait, he did not hesitate, and he did not pause. He reached out and sought Gods when he was faced with his trials and tribulations.

It is a good object lesson for all of us. Too often, we lean on our own power, wisdom and strength to solve our problems; instead, we should be leaning into God and bringing our prayers and petitions to Him.

Stop now and take time to list out the things you want reach out to God and bring to Him. Here are some common issues to pray about right now:

- Relationships
  - Family
    - Children
    - Parents
    - Extended Family
  - Friends
  - Neighbors
- Physical
- Work
- Finances
- Material Needs

No matter the need or circumstance – bring it to God in prayer right now!

Hannah

In Hannah we have a character who is daily maligned, scorned and ridiculed by her rival because she has no children and her womb is closed.

Hannah went to the temple to pray and pour her heart out to God. What I love about her prayer is that only God heard it. She did not verbalize her pray, but was speaking it in her heart and mind.

Eli the priest was watching her lips move (he thought she was drunk), but she was praying in her heart. This is so beautiful to know that God knows our heart and mind. We do not have to speak the words aloud for our God to hear us! Our heart can cry out and the God of this universe is there to hear that cry.

Think about that! You can be in a meeting, in your car, with a group of people, or in your quiet place and no matter where you are, you can lift a pray to God in your heart and mind at that very moment and God is there to listen and hear.

Remember Hannah and her petition the next time you feel the need to pray, but cannot make a sound.   God will hear you!

1 Samuel 1: 12-18

Now it came about, as she continued praying before the Lord, that Eli was watching her mouth. As for Hannah, she was speaking in her heart, only her lips were moving, but her voice was not heard. So Eli thought she was drunk. Then Eli said to her, "How long will you make yourself drunk? Put away your wine from you." But Hannah replied, "No, my lord, I am a woman oppressed in spirit; I have drunk neither wine nor strong drink, but I have poured out my soul before the Lord. Do not consider your maidservant as a worthless woman, for I have spoken until now out of my great concern and provocation." Then Eli answered and said, "Go in peace; and may the God of Israel grant your petition that you have asked of Him." She said, "Let your maidservant find favor in your sight." So the woman went her way and ate, and her face was no longer sad.

The Psalms

I love the Psalms because I can see myself in the same place as these writers. It brings me great comfort to know that others have gone before me and cried out to God and God answered them.

There are so many great psalms to consider when you are in times of trouble and distress. In all of the verses below see how the Psalmist cried out in times of trouble

The psalmist used phrases like the following to describe their situation. Can you relate to any of these?

- **In the day of my trouble**
- **I will cry aloud**
- **From my Distress**
- **For I am lonely and afflicted.**
- **Let my cry for help**
- **For I am afflicted and needy**
- **When I cry to You for help**

These were not people who were just a suffering a little, these were folks who were suffering a lot! They were literally crying out to God and bringing their prayers and supplications, wants and needs to the mighty God of our universe. As you read the verses that follow, know that we have a gracious heavenly father who hears our prayers and knows our needs. Know that you are not alone and that others have gone before you.

Psalm 120:1

In my trouble I cried to the Lord,…

Psalm 107:6

Then they cried out to the Lord in their trouble;….

Psalm 77:1-2

My voice rises to God, and I will cry aloud;
My voice rises to God, and He will hear me.
In the day of my trouble I sought the Lord;
In the night my hand was stretched out without weariness;
My soul refused to be comforted.

Psalm 118:5

From my distress I called upon the Lord;....

Psalm 25:16-17

Turn to me and be gracious to me,
For I am lonely and afflicted.
The troubles of my heart are enlarged;
Bring me out of my distresses.

Psalm 102:1-2

Hear my prayer, O Lord!
And let my cry for help come to You.
Do not hide Your face from me in the day of my distress;
Incline Your ear to me;
In the day when I call answer me quickly.

Psalm 86:1

Incline Your ear, O Lord, and answer me;
For I am afflicted and needy.

Psalm 61:1

Hear my cry, O God;
Give heed to my prayer.

Psalm 55:1

Give ear to my prayer, O God;
And do not hide Yourself from my supplication.

Psalm 70:5

But I am afflicted and needy;
Hasten to me, O God!
You are my help and my deliverer;
O Lord, do not delay.

Psalm 28:2

Hear the voice of my supplications when I cry to You for help,
When I lift up my hands toward Your holy sanctuary.

Psalm 86:6-7

Give ear, O Lord, to my prayer;
And give heed to the voice of my supplications!
In the day of my trouble I shall call upon You,
For You will answer me.

Psalm 142:1-2

I cry aloud with my voice to the Lord;
I make supplication with my voice to the Lord.
I pour out my complaint before Him;
I declare my trouble before Him.

Before I wrote this book, I was not a great student of the Psalms. I always spent most of my time in Proverbs on a daily basis. However, I have come to realize how powerful and beautiful the psalms are and how they speak to my heart, mind, body and soul.

I pray you will take the time to become a student of the Psalms and not just a reader of the Psalms.

Now that we have seen how the Psalmist cried out to God, let see how God answered those prayers.

How God Answers Those Who Pray in Psalms

Now let's see how God answered when people cried out to Him:

God is always listening! He never sleeps, he never slumbers, and He is good father who only wants the best for his children. His ears are open and his eyes are constantly seeking.

Psalm 50:15

Call upon Me in the day of trouble; I shall rescue you, and you will honor Me."

Psalm 3:4

And He answered me from His holy mountain.   Selah.

Psalm 118:5

The Lord answered me and set me in a large place.

Psalm 107:6

He delivered them out of their distresses.

Psalm 138:3

On the day I called, You answered me; You made me bold with strength in my soul.

Psalm 120:1

In my trouble I cried to the Lord, And He answered me.

Psalm 34:4

I sought the Lord, and He answered me, And delivered me from all my fears.

Psalm 28:6

Blessed be the Lord,
Because He has heard the voice of my supplication.

Psalm 145:18-19

The Lord is near to all who call upon Him,
To all who call upon Him in truth.
He will fulfill the desire of those who fear Him;
He will also hear their cry and will save them.

Psalm 34:15

The eyes of the Lord are toward the righteous
And His ears are open to their cry.

So in all of the verses from Psalms where we see God answering. What were the answers?

- **Deliverance and rescue**
- **Set in a large place**
- **Fulfilled desire**
- **Boldness**
- **Strength**

These are exactly the things we need when we call out to God in our distress and times of trouble.

We can now exam the following questions

Q. When is the right time to pray?

Q. Where is the right place to pray?

Q. Our posture during prayer?

When to Pray

So when should we pray? Is there one time of day that is better than another? Is there a day of the week or month of the year that will be better for us to offer our prayers to God?   Of course not!   God is constantly there to hear our prayers and petitions.

Pray in the morning – Psalm 5:3, Mark 1:35, Psalm 88:13

For many people, starting the day with prayer is the best way to begin each day. Before the cares of the world start to burden your shoulders and weigh you down, you can start your day in communion with God.

Psalm 5:3

In the morning, O Lord, You will hear my voice;
In the morning I will order my prayer to You and eagerly watch.

Mark 1:35

In the early morning, while it was still dark, Jesus got up, left the house, and went away to a secluded place, and was praying there.

Psalm 88:13

But I, O Lord, have cried out to You for help,
And in the morning my prayer comes before You.

Pray at noon – Acts 10:9

Perhaps a break at mid-day would be the most appropriate time for you to catch up with God. Below, you can see that Peter went to his roof to pray at the 6th hour (noon). As your day progresses, you can take some time to reflect and pray to God and thank Him for His many blessings as well seeking guidance for the remainder of the day.

Acts 10:9

On the next day, as they were on their way and approaching the city, Peter went up on the housetop about the sixth hour to pray.

Pray at night – Acts 16:25, Luke 6:12, Psalm119:62

As the day closes you can reflect and talk to God about what has transpired and what is to come in the next day. Perhaps you cannot sleep or you are weary. Taking your cares and burdens to the Lord is a great way to help ease your mind and relax your body as you prepare for rest.

Acts 16:25

But about midnight Paul and Silas were praying and singing hymns of praise to God, and the prisoners were listening to them;

Luke 6:12

It was at this time that He went off to the mountain to pray, and He spent the whole night in prayer to God.

Psalm 119:62

*At midnight I shall rise to give thanks to You
Because of Your righteous ordinances.*

Pray several times per day – Daniel 6:10

Daniel is being held in captivity, but he has not forgotten his God and how he was raised by his parents. Even though his is a virtual prisoner in a foreign land, Daniel continues to give thanks to God. He is wise enough to realize the he serves a mighty God who is the author of all creation and circumstances and is worthy of our praise.

Daniel 6:10

Now when Daniel knew that the document was signed, he entered his house (now in his roof chamber he had windows open toward Jerusalem); and he continued kneeling on his knees three times a day, praying and giving thanks before his God, as he had been doing previously.

Pray without ceasing – 1 Thessalonians 5:17, Ephesians 6:18

Does this really mean to pray all the time! You bet it does. I take this literally and have some of my best "conversations" with God during my day.

I have an hour long commute to work and frequently leave very early before there is much traffic. I take advantage of this time to offer up my prayer and praise to God. It is sweet time alone with the Lord with few distractions and the opportunity to pray about anything and everything.

I also run each day and frequently take this time to pray and praise God. There have been several times when I have been broken hearted and went for a run to clear my head and heart and have poured out my feelings and thoughts to God. I have literally stopped running and started weeping – sometimes in praise and sometimes in pain, but always in an attitude of prayer.

1 Thessalonians 5:17

pray without ceasing;

Ephesians 6:18

With all prayer and petition pray at all times in the Spirit, and with this in view, be on the alert with all perseverance and petition for all the saints,

To recap, there is no specific "good time or proper time" to pray to God. We can offer our prayers anytime!

- **Pray in the morning**
- **Pray at noon**
- **Pray at night**
- **Pray several times per day**
- **Pray without ceasing**

Where to Pray

As you read in the previous chapter there was not a specific "good time" to pray to God. Anytime is a good time to pray to the Lord. In the same way, you will see there is not a specific "place" to pray. God can hear us no matter our location.

In Church (Temple) – Acts 3:1, 1 Kings 8:22, Luke 18:10

2 Chronicles 7:11-16

Thus Solomon finished the house of the Lord and the king's palace, and successfully completed all that he had planned on doing in the house of the Lord and in his palace.

Then the Lord appeared to Solomon at night and said to him, "I have heard your prayer and have chosen this place for Myself as a house of sacrifice. If I shut up the heavens so that there is no rain, or if I command the locust to devour the land, or if I send pestilence among My people, and My people who are called by My name humble themselves and pray and seek My face and turn from their wicked ways, then I will hear from heaven, will forgive their sin and will heal their land. Now My eyes will be open and My ears attentive to the prayer offered in this place. For now I have chosen and consecrated this house that My name may be there forever, and My eyes and My heart will be there perpetually.

1 Kings 8:22-23

Then Solomon stood before the altar of the Lord in the presence of all the assembly of Israel and spread out his hands toward heaven. He said, "O Lord, the God of Israel, there is no God like You in heaven above or on earth beneath, keeping covenant and showing lovingkindness to Your servants who walk before You with all their heart,

Acts 3:1

Now Peter and John were going up to the temple at the ninth hour, the hour of prayer.

There is just something special about praying in church with other believers. In fact, the Bible tells us – "when two or more are gathered together, God is their midst".   Being church allows you to share your prayer requests with others as well as to offer encouragement and pray for others.

Matthew 18:20

For where two or three have gathered together in My name, I am there in their midst."

At Home – Daniel 6:10

Daniel 6:10

Now when Daniel knew that the document was signed, he entered his house (now in his roof chamber he had windows open toward Jerusalem); and he continued kneeling on his knees three times a day, praying and giving thanks before his God, as he had been doing previously.

Home is where we should be doing the vast majority of or praying. In the morning before work and in the evening before falling asleep   We should be leading our family in prayer and offering up the example of prayer to our spouse and children.

In secret – Matthew 6:6

Matthew 6:6

But you, when you pray, go into your inner room, close your door and pray to your Father who is in secret, and your Father who sees what is done in secret will reward you.

Do you have a special place to pray? Where it is quiet and you can pour out yourself to God. If not, then try to find that place.

Riverside – Acts 16:13

Acts 16:13

And on the Sabbath day we went outside the gate to a riverside, where we were supposing that there would be a place of prayer; and we sat down and began speaking to the women who had assembled.

In a Secluded place – Mark 1:35

Mark 1:35

In the early morning, while it was still dark, Jesus got up, left the house, and went away to a secluded place, and was praying there.

On A Mountain Top – Luke 6:12, Mark 6:46

Luke 6:12

It was at this time that He went off to the mountain to pray, and He spent the whole night in prayer to God.

Mark 6:46
After bidding them farewell, He left for the mountain to pray.

On a Roof – Acts 10:9

Acts 10:9

On the next day, as they were on their way and approaching the city, Peter went up on the housetop about the sixth hour to pray.

In the Wilderness – Luke 5:16

Luke 5:16

But Jesus Himself would often slip away to the wilderness and pray.

In a Fish's Belly - Jonah 2:1-2

Jonah 2:1-2

*Then Jonah prayed to the Lord his God from the stomach of the fish, and he said,
"I called out of my distress to the Lord, And He answered me.
I cried for help from the depth of Sheol; You heard my voice.*

Everywhere – 1 Timothy 2:8

1 Timothy 2:8

*Therefore I want the men in every place to pray, lifting up holy hands, without
wrath and dissension.*

It is clear from scripture that people prayed anywhere and everywhere.
Below is a brief recap of all of the different places people prayed.

In Church (Temple) – Acts 3:1, 1 Kings 8:22, Luke 18:10

At Home– Daniel 6:10

In secret – Matthew 6:6

Riverside – Acts 16:13

On A Mountain Top– Luke 6:12, Mark 6:46

In a Secluded place – Mark 1:35

On a Roof – Acts 10:9

In the Wilderness – Luke 5:16

In a Fish's Belly - Jonah 2:1-2

Everywhere – 1 Timothy 2:8

It really does not matter where you are physically located to offer up prayer. God is with you no matter the location. That is the real beauty of prayer and talking with God. It can be done anywhere. Why not take the time this week to seek out a new place to pray and talk to God. Take the example of Christ and seek out a quiet and secluded place. Choose to be still and listen to God in the quiet of the moment.

Posture of Prayer

When you think about the posture of prayer, what position comes to mind? For me I thought about prayer on my knees with head bowed before God.

As I examined the Bible, I found there was no specific "posture" for prayer. God is not as concerned with the posture of your body as He is concerned with the posture of your heart!

Sitting – 2 Samuel 7:18

2 Samuel 7:18

Then David the king went in and sat before the Lord, and he said, "Who am I, O Lord God, and what is my house, that You have brought me this far?

Some of my best prayer times have been on my long commute to work early in the morning. My office if an hour away from my home and leaving at 5:00 am allows me to not only beat traffic, but also have some long conversations with God.

Lifting Hands – 1 Timothy 2:8

1 Timothy 2:8

Therefore I want the men in every place to pray, lifting up holy hands, without wrath and dissension.

I used to be one of those people who did not understand others who lifted their hands in prayer and praise. Until God got ahold of my heart and I would spontaneously lift my hands to God in prayer. I usually do this when I am outside in the woods or on a hike and I am overwhelmed by the beauty and majesty around me. I cannot help but lift my arms to God in prayer.

Face Down – Numbers 20:6

Numbers 20:6

Then Moses and Aaron came in from the presence of the assembly to the doorway of the tent of meeting and fell on their faces. Then the glory of the Lord appeared to them;

Many times when I have approached God in prayer it has been with my face down, not worthy of forgiveness and mercy, but seeking redemption and confessing my sins, knowing God is a just and loving God who is quick to forgive and offer mercy and grace.

Looking Up – John 17:1

John 17:1

Jesus spoke these things; and lifting up His eyes to heaven, He said, "Father, the hour has come; glorify Your Son, that the Son may glorify You,

Lying Down – Psalm 63:6

Psalm 63:6

When I remember You on my bed, I meditate on You in the night watches,

How many nights did I lie in bed and offer up prayer to the mighty King of Glory! Sometimes it was because of a bad dream, other times my heart was overflowing with joy, but many times it was because my mind was filled with anger or sadness and I need to speak with God and talk with Him about my troubles and sorrows. Instead of tossing and turning, I spent the time in prayer. It was a much better use of time.

Prostrate (lying on the ground face down) – Matthew 26:39

Matthew 26:39

And He went a little beyond them, and fell on His face and prayed, saying, "My Father, if it is possible, let this cup pass from Me; yet not as I will, but as You will."

Bowing Down – Psalm 95:6

Psalm 95:6

Come, let us worship and bow down,
Let us kneel before the Lord our Maker.

Kneeling – Daniel 6:10, Luke 22:41, 2 Chronicles 6:13, 1 Kings 8:54

Daniel 6:10

Now when Daniel knew that the document was signed, he entered his house (now in his roof chamber he had windows open toward Jerusalem); and he continued kneeling on his knees three times a day, praying and giving thanks before his God, as he had been doing previously.

Standing – 2 Chronicles 20:5-6, 2 Chronicles 20:13, Genesis 24:12-14, 1 Samuel 1:26, 1 Kings 8:22, Mark 11:25

Mark 11:25

Whenever you stand praying, forgive, if you have anything against anyone, so that your Father who is in heaven will also forgive you your transgressions.

What God desires is that we bring our prayers and petitions to Him. As you saw in the verses before, there are many different postures of prayer and no matter the posture, God is there and He is listening. Remember, God is more concerned about the posture of your heart than your physical posture!

Below is a brief recap on one page of all of the different postures.

Sitting– 2 Samuel 7:18

Lifting Hands – 1 Timothy 2:8

Face Down – Numbers 20:6

Looking Up – John 17:1

Lying Down - Psalm 63:6

Prostrate – Matthew 26:39

Bowing Down – Psalm 95:6

Kneeling - Daniel 6:10, Luke 22:41, 2 Chronicles 6:13, 1 Kings 8:54

Standing- 2 Chronicles 20:5-6, 2 Chronicles 20:13,   Genesis 24:12-14, 1 Samuel 1:26, 1 Kings 8:22, Mark 11:25

Prayer Recap

Let me recap the fundamentals of prayer in this book

1. Why Pray – because it is effective and God is listening
2. When should we pray – all the time!
3. Where should we pray – anywhere!
4. What should our posture be when we pray? It does not matter!
   God can hear your prayers no matter the position of you body. It
   is the posture of your heart the matters

You see, too many people make prayer much too complicated.   It is not
complicated at all! God can hear your prayer. Consider this poem:

From the highest mountain,
To the deepest sea,
From the belly of a fish,
To a jail cell at midnight,
From the middle of a storm,
To the quiet of an olive orchard at night,
In the face of a blazing furnace,
Or in the face of those with stones in their hands,
From a lions den,
Or before a giant in the land,
From a cave when you are being pursed,
To the temple before the people,
Eyes open,
Eyes closed,
Hands held high,
Head bowed down,
Sitting up,
Laying down,
Morning, noon and night
Rain or Shine
24/7/365
Pray!

A.C.T.S.
Praying

A-C-T-S praying is just any easy acronym for learning how to pray to God. After I learned this simple method, I have been using it ever since.

It works like this, you start your prayer with A and work through the letter – A-C-T-S

A = Adoration or Praise

C = Confession

T = Thanksgiving

S = Supplication or Intercession

Adoration and Praise

Starting your prayer with adoration and praise is our way of acknowledging God for who He is and for his greatness. The Psalmist did an excellent job of praising God. Consider the verses below from King David and how beautifully he praises God.

Psalm 8:1

O Lord, our Lord, how majestic is your name in all the earth,
Who have displayed your splendor above the heavens!

In Psalms I looked for all the things the writers had to say about God as they cried out to him in their prayers and supplications. If you are looking for descriptions of God with which you can praise Him, then consider personalizing each of these phrases.

You are my - Creator
You are my - Defender
You are my - Deliverer
You are my - Shield
You are my - Salvation
You are my - Shelter
You are my - Strength
You are my - Shepard
You are my - Sanctuary
You are my - Stronghold
You are my - Refuge
You are my - Rock
You are my - Rescuer
You are my – Rest
You are my – Resting place
You are my - Protector
You are my – Promise Keeper
You are my - Fortress
You are my - Light
You are my - Light in the darkness
You are my - Helper
You are my – Healer
You are my – Hope
You are my – Portion
You are my - Vindicator
You are my - My Confidence
You are - A very present help
You are – The bearer of my burdens

What a great way to start you prayer with the acknowledgment of all God is, has been and will be in your life!

When you think about God and how to offer praise and adoration, you should also think about the character of God and offer praise and adoration for those characteristics.

- **God is Holy**   1 Peter 1:15, Isaiah 6:3
- **God never changes** Psalm 33:11, James 1:17, Hebrews 13:8
- **God is Love**   Psalm 100:5, Ephesians 3:17-18.
- **God is Just**   Jeremiah 17:10, Deuteronomy 32:4
- **God is Merciful**   James 5:11, Hebrews 4:16
- **God is Faithful**   Psalm 89:8, 1 Peter 4:19
- **God is Sovereign**   1 Chronicles 29:11, 12, Job 12:10
- **God is Omnipotent (He is all powerful)**   Jeremiah 32:17
- **God is Omnipresent (He is everywhere)**   Psalm 139:7-10
- **God is Omniscient (He knows everything)** Romans 11:33, 34

As you contemplate your prayers, take time to study these scriptures and get to know the character of God. This will then translate to you being able to offer praise and adoration to God no matter your circumstances or condition.

Confession

As important as it is to offer adoration and praise, we must also come to God with a clean heart and confess our sins and trespasses. Consider the example we have from Daniel and Nehemiah. See below how they offer praise and adoration to God and then offer confession for a multitude of transgressions the people have committed. God desires us to be holy in our lives.

Daniel 9:4-5

I prayed to the Lord my God and confessed and said, "Alas, O Lord, the great and awesome God, who keeps His covenant and lovingkindness for those who love Him and keep His commandments, we have sinned, committed iniquity, acted wickedly and rebelled, even turning aside from Your commandments and ordinances.

Nehemiah 1:5-7

I said, "I beseech You, O Lord God of heaven, the great and awesome God, who preserves the covenant and lovingkindness for those who love Him and keep His commandments, let Your ear now be attentive and Your eyes open to hear the prayer of Your servant which I am praying before You now, day and night, on behalf of the sons of Israel Your servants, confessing the sins of the sons of Israel which we have sinned against You; I and my father's house have sinned. 7 We have acted very corruptly against You and have not kept the commandments, nor the statutes, nor the ordinances which You commanded Your servant Moses.

God will not hear the prayer of those who do not confess and acknowledge their waywardness.

Proverbs 28:9

He who turns away his ear from listening to the law,
Even his prayer is an abomination.

1 John 1:9-10

If we confess our sins, He is faithful and righteous to forgive us our sins and to cleanse us from all unrighteousness. If we say that we have not sinned, we make Him a liar and His word is not in us.

Confession of sin is not only good for the heart, mind and soul, it is also good for the body. Consider the words from David as he wrote this Psalm:

Psalm 32:3-7

When I kept silent about my sin, my body wasted away
Through my groaning all day long.
For day and night Your hand was heavy upon me;
My vitality was drained away as with the fever heat of summer.   Selah.
I acknowledged my sin to You,
And my iniquity I did not hide;
I said, "I will confess my transgressions to the Lord";
And You forgave the guilt of my sin.   Selah.
Therefore, let everyone who is godly pray to You in a time when You may be found;
Surely in a flood of great waters they will not reach him.
You are my hiding place; You preserve me from trouble;
You surround me with songs of deliverance.   Selah.

Thanksgiving

Thanksgiving is the attitude we should bring when we are offering our prayers to God. Thanksgiving is all about what God had done and will do for us.

Colossians 4:2

Devote yourselves to prayer, keeping alert in it with an attitude of thanksgiving;

Philippians 4:6

Be anxious for nothing, but in everything by prayer and supplication with thanksgiving let your requests be made known to God.

1 Thessalonians 5:16-18

Rejoice always; pray without ceasing; in everything give thanks; for this is God's will for you in Christ Jesus.

Ephesians 5:20

always giving thanks for all things in the name of our Lord Jesus Christ to God, even the Father;

Supplication and Intercession

Supplication is humbly asking for something (usually for ourselves) and intercession is asking on the behalf of others. When we bring our prayers and petitions to God, not only do we ask for our own needs, but we can also beseech God for others.

Philippians 4:6

Be anxious for nothing, but in everything by prayer and supplication with thanksgiving let your requests be made known to God.

James 5:16
Therefore, confess your sins to one another, and pray for one another so that you may be healed. The effective prayer of a righteous man can accomplish much.

Now that you know the A-C-T-S way to pray, I hope you will put this to use in your prayer life.

A = Adoration or Praise

C = Confession

T = Thanksgiving

S = Supplication or Intercession

Types of Prayer

There are many different types of prayer we find in the Bible. You are probably familiar with the most basic forms of prayer:

- Praying for ourselves
- Praying for others
- Prayers of thanks
- Prayer of praise

While these are the most basic forms of prayers, the Bible teaches us that there are many different prayers. Study each of these different prayers and know there are many ways to approach God in prayer. Which is the best prayer? It depends of your circumstances and situation.

Prayer of Supplication (also known as prayer of petition)

The prayer of supplication is probably the most common prayer we offer up to God. These are the prayers we bring asking for both the large and small things we need God's help with. Here are some common things we pray for – good health, safety, daily provision, wisdom, discernment, relationships, etc.

You can see in the verse below we are called to bring EVERYTHING in prayer. It is a call to faith and trust that we bring these things to God!

Philippians 4:6

Be anxious for nothing, but in everything by prayer and supplication with thanksgiving let your requests be made known to God.

Luke 11:9-13

"So I say to you, ask, and it will be given to you; seek, and you will find; knock, and it will be opened to you. For everyone who asks, receives; and he who seeks, finds; and to him who knocks, it will be opened. Now suppose one of you fathers is asked by his son for a fish; he will not give him a snake instead of a fish, will he? Or if he is asked for an egg, he will not give him a scorpion, will he? If you then, being evil, know how to give good gifts to your children, how much more will your heavenly Father give the Holy Spirit to those who ask Him?"

Prayer of intercession (praying for others)

Intercessory prayers are the prayers we bring to God on behalf of others. These can be prayers for people we know well (family and friends), or prayers for strangers and people we just met. Intercessory prayers are the most unselfish prayers and should be a part of your regular repertoire. Commit to having a prayer journal and lifting others to God in prayer.

Here are some people you can consistently pray for:

- Family & Friends
- Co-workers
- Pastor/Preacher/Church Members
- Neighbors
- Teachers
- Government Leaders (National, State & Local)
- Military and others who serves us

1 Timothy 2:1

First of all, then, I urge that entreaties and prayers, petitions and thanksgivings, be made on behalf of all men,

Romans 8:31-34

What then shall we say to these things? If God is for us, who is against us? He who did not spare His own Son, but delivered Him over for us all, how will He not also with Him freely give us all things? Who will bring a charge against God's elect? God is the one who justifies; who is the one who condemns? Christ Jesus is He who died, yes, rather who was raised, who is at the right hand of God, who also intercedes for us.

Ephesians 1:15-18

For this reason I too, having heard of the faith in the Lord Jesus which exists among you and your love for all the saints, do not cease giving thanks for you, while making mention of you in my prayers; that the God of our Lord Jesus Christ, the Father of glory, may give to you a spirit of wisdom and of revelation in the knowledge of Him. I pray that the eyes of your heart may be enlightened, so that you will know what is the hope of His calling, what are the riches of the glory of His inheritance in the saints,

Prayer of agreement (sometimes called corporate prayer)

The prayer of agreement or corporate prayer is just a common prayer that a group of fellow believers bring to God as a group. This is usually done in conjunction with intercessory prayer. You will often find a group of believer coming together to pray for the sick or those who are in distress. It is a beautiful and wonderful thing to see many people gathered together and praying together.

The prayer of agreement can also be prayed daily in your own home! As a family, my Bride will gather the kids in the morning and pray with them and in the evening I will gather the whole family together and we will bring our prayers and petitions to God.

You can also have this prayer of agreement in the workplace. I have had several occasions when there were opportunities to gather with fellow believers to lift up our prayers. As you can see in the verse below, it is when two or more are gathered together, we can offer up the prayer of agreement.

Matthew 18:19-20

"Again I say to you, that if two of you agree on earth about anything that they may ask, it shall be done for them by My Father who is in heaven. For where two or three have gathered together in My name, I am there in their midst."

Acts 2:42

They were continually devoting themselves to the apostles' teaching and to fellowship, to the breaking of bread and to prayer.

Prayer of thanksgiving

What do you have to be thankful for? Can't think of anything? Here are a few things I am thankful for as I write this chapter. I do praise God for these things I am thankful for his love and mercy! What is on your list?

- Jesus
- My beautiful Bride
- Children
- Bible
- Church fellowship
- Food
- Clothing
- Shelter
- Job
- Ability to walk, talk, see, taste, hear and smell
- Friends
- Family
- Transportation
- Ability to think and reason
- Computer to write this book
- Peace and Tranquillity in my home
- Freedom to worship in USA

Psalm 95:2-3

Let us come before His presence with thanksgiving,
Let us shout joyfully to Him with psalms.
For the Lord is a great God
And a great King above all gods,

Psalm 100:4-5

Enter His gates with thanksgiving
And His courts with praise.
Give thanks to Him, bless His name.
For the Lord is good;
His lovingkindness is everlasting
And His faithfulness to all generations.

Prayer of consecration (or prayer of dedication)

Consecration is defined as the solemn dedication to a special purpose or service. This is a special prayer when we can use when we are preparing a special work or service to God. See below how Jesus commits himself to God's ultimate will and purpose.

Matthew 26:39

And He (Jesus) went a little beyond them, and fell on His face and prayed, saying, "My Father, if it is possible, let this cup pass from Me; yet not as I will, but as You will."

Luke 22:42

saying, "Father, if You are willing, remove this cup from Me; yet not My will, but Yours be done."

Prayer of imprecation - (praying for judgement)

In the Psalms you can find several prayers of imprecation (this is basically of prayer that God will curse your enemy). Read Psalm 7, Psalm 55, and Psalm 69 and you will see how David is reaching out to God to protect him and bring destruction to his enemy.

However, we must juxtapose this prayer of imprecation with what Jesus teaches us in Matthew about loving our enemy:

Matthew 5:44-45

But I say to you, love your enemies and pray for those who persecute you, so that you may be sons of your Father who is in heaven; for He causes His sun to rise on the evil and the good, and sends rain on the righteous and the unrighteous.

Luke 6:27-29

"But I say to you who hear, love your enemies, do good to those who hate you, bless those who curse you, pray for those who mistreat you. Whoever hits you on the cheek, offer him the other also; and whoever takes away your coat, do not withhold your shirt from him either.

Praying in the Spirit

This verse means so much to me! I distinctly remember a time in my life when there was a severe family trial and I was in my office in the basement literally crying out to God and praying. At one point, I could offer no more words. I literally started groaning and in my heart I was pleading with God. I know He heard the prayer of this father that day and it was not me, but the Holy Spirit making intercession for me.

Romans 8:26-27

In the same way the Spirit also helps our weakness; for we do not know how to pray as we should, but the Spirit Himself intercedes for us with groanings too deep for words; and He who searches the hearts knows what the mind of the Spirit is, because He intercedes for the saints according to the will of God.

Prayer of confession

It is important that we acknowledge and ask forgiveness of our sins. Every sin is a sin against God, therefore it is important that we call out to God and ask for His forgiveness. I love that God promises to forgive and cleanse us when we confess our sins.

As we discussed in the previous chapter, confession should be a part of regular conversation with God. You cannot hide your sins or transgression from God, so it is better to make this a consistent part of your prayer routine.

1 John 1:9

If we confess our sins, He is faithful and righteous to forgive us our sins and to cleanse us from all unrighteousness.

James 5:16

Therefore, confess your sins to one another, and pray for one another so that you may be healed. The effective prayer of a righteous man can accomplish much.

Below is a brief recap of the different types of prayer we find in the Bible.

Prayer of Supplication (also known as prayer of petition)

Prayer of intercession (praying for others)

Prayer of agreement (sometimes called corporate prayer)

Prayer of thanksgiving

Prayer of consecration (or prayer of dedication)

Prayer of imprecation (prayer of judgement)

Praying in the Spirit

Prayer of confession

Barriers to Prayer

A good friend of mine by the name of Preston Poore is writing a book and had asked me to review and comment on it for him. The book is called:

"The Discipled Leader - Become an Extraordinary Christian & Change the World." It is an excellent book that lays out how we as Christians should lead our lives and become true Disciples of Jesus Christ.

In that book, he had several pages on Barriers to Prayer that I thought were really good and I asked his permission to include them as a chapter in this book. He was kind enough to allow me to include them.

Barriers to Prayer
Our prayers might be unproductive or ineffective at times; it can feel like they don't go beyond the ceiling. There might be many reasons for this, including the following:

• **Pride:** This is the root of all other sins. It is putting us before God and being independent from him. R. C. Sproul wrote, "One of the things that betrays our fallen condition is the concept of the self-made man, one who takes credit for the bounty of his goods and forgets the source of all his provision. We must remember that God gives us all we have in the ultimate sense."[138] Supplementing this thought, John MacArthur wrote in his book *Alone with God*, "Christians can actually behave like practical humanists, living as if God were not necessary. When that happens, passionate longing for God and yearning for his help will be missing — along with his empowerment."[139] When we are filled with pride, our prayers will be hindered.

• **Ingratitude:** This is the exact opposite of appreciation. It is forgetting God and what he's done in our lives. It leads to not thanking God; not expressing our gratitude. In Luke 17, Jesus tells a parable about ten lepers who were healed; while all ten were probably grateful for the healing, only one returned to actually thank him. Let's remember to thank God and not allow our hearts to be hardened by forgetting.

• **Unresolved Conflicts:** Our relationship with others matters to God. If there is tension, bitterness, hatred, anger, or resentment between us and someone else, it is up to us to seek resolution and forgive others before approaching God. Jesus said, "This how I want you to conduct yourself in these matters. If you enter your place of worship and, about to make an offering, you suddenly remember a grudge a friend has against you, abandon your offering, leave immediately, go to this friend, and make things right. Then and only then, come back and work things out with God" (Matthew 5:23–24 The Message). It is an insult to God for us to withhold forgiveness and grace from those who ask us, while claiming to be forgiven and saved by grace ourselves. We ought to remember that "forgiven people forgive other people."[140] So, before we seek God in prayer, let's resolve outstanding conflicts to avoid any barriers.

• **Marital Discord:** If we're married, God takes notice of how we treat our spouses. If there is friction and arguments between married couples, the conflict interrupts their relationship. Treating our spouses with honor and dignity, loving them the way Christ loved the church produces unity; conflict produces separation. The Bible says, "Husbands, in the same way be considerate as you live with your wives, and treat them with respect as the weaker partner and as heirs with you of the gracious gift of life, so that nothing will hinder your prayers" (1 Pet. 3:7 NIV). Marital discord will interrupt and impede our prayers. Let's determine to treat our spouses well and God will hear our prayers.

The bottom line is that sin creates a barrier to our prayers. It can be sin against God or sin against others. A key part of our walk with God is realizing that sin obstructs our interaction with him, and confession will open the lines of communication with him. With all of this said, one of the biggest barriers to prayer is anxiety.

Don't Be Anxious

Often, we are filled with worry, anxiety, and stress. We allow circumstances to drain our lives of joy and peace. It's kind of like dominos; worry leads to anxiety and anxiety leads to stress. How do they work together to threaten our well-being?

• **Worry** is "to subject to persistent or nagging attention or effort."[141] Furthermore, worry "implies an incessant goading or attacking that drives one to desperation."[142]

• **Anxiety** is "an abnormal and overwhelming sense of apprehension and fear often marked by physiological signs (such as sweating, tension, and increased pulse), by doubt concerning the reality and nature of the threat, and by self-doubt about one's capacity to cope with it."[143] Anxiety is a behavioral response to worry.

• When we worry about uncertainties we become anxious and stressed. The problem of anxiety is rampant and it drains mental, physical, and spiritual energy; the health costs can be great because of the following factors:[144]

• Forty million people in the U.S. will experience impairment because of an anxiety condition this year.

• Only four million will receive treatment, and of those, only four hundred thousand will receive proper treatment.

• Those who experience anxiety and stress have a very high propensity for drug abuse and addictions.

• 65 percent of North Americans take prescription medications daily; 4 percent take mood-altering prescriptions regularly.

• Recreational drugs are also used to cope with anxiety. 42 percent of young adults in America regularly use recreational drugs (National Institute on Drug Abuse).

• Alcohol is commonly used to cope with anxiety.

• 25–40 percent of all patients in U.S. hospitals are being treated for complications resulting from alcohol-related problems (The Marin Institute).

• Alcohol-related car crashes are the number-one killer of teens. Alcohol use is also associated with homicides, suicides, and drowning's — the next three leading causes of death among youth (Center for Substance Abuse Prevention).

Clearly, people are looking to medicate themselves, become numb, and escape the anxiety in their lives. They are seeking peace, rest, and ease. "The great enemy of peace is anxiety."[145]

Anxiety has a huge impact on our lives and our relationship with God. For the human race, anxiety is a complex issue. For the Christian, it is a simpler issue and can be handled through trusting in God. We are not to be filled with anxiety and tossed without care. "Rather, we are to bring our problems and needs to the Lord with the confidence that he cares for us and his care is sufficient."[146]

The life of a Christian who is walking with God and trusting in him is marked by peace. Peace is the enemy of anxiety. Warren Wiersbe wrote, "Peace is the inner tranquility and confidence that God is in control. This does not mean the absence of trials on the outside, but it does mean a quiet confidence within, regardless of circumstances, people, or things."[147]

Additionally, theologian Matthew Henry wrote, "This peace will *keep our hearts and minds through Christ Jesus;* it will keep us from sinning under our troubles, and from sinking under them; keep us calm and sedate, without discomposure of passion, and with inward satisfaction."[148]

In Dale Carnegie's book, *How to Stop Worrying and Start Living*, he outlined very practical advice on how to handle worry:

1. Pray.
2. Ask yourself, "What is the worst that can possibly happen?"
3. Prepare to accept it if you have to.
4. Then calmly proceed to improve upon the worst.

I strongly believe that anxiety, worry, and stress can be overcome by trusting in God, turning everything over to him in prayer, and acting as Dale Carnegie suggests. Through these things, God's peace will fill you and enable you to handle any circumstance.

Source:

139 MacArthur, J. F., Jr. Alone with God. Wheaton, IL: Victor Books, 1995, p. 14.

140 Sproul, R. C. *Does Prayer Change Things?* Lake Mary, FL: Reformation Trust Publishing, 2009, Vol. 3, p. 37.

141 Mish, F. C. Preface, *Merriam-Webster's Collegiate Dictionary.* (Eleventh ed.). Springfield, MA:Merriam-Webster, Inc, 2003.

142 Ibid.

143 Ibid.

144 anxietycentre.com.

145 Utley, R. J. *Paul Bound, the Gospel Unbound: Letters from Prison (Colossians, Ephesians and Philemon, then later, Philippians).* Marshall, TX: Bible Lessons International, 1997, Volume 8.

146 Ellsworth, R. *Opening Up Philippians.* Leominster: Day One Publications, 2004, p. 84. 172

147 Wiersbe, *The Bible Exposition Commentary.* Wheaton, IL: Victor Books, 1996, Vol. 2, p. 95.

148 Henry, M., *Matthew Henry's Commentary on the Whole Bible: Complete and Unabridged in One Volume.* Peabody, MA: Hendrickson, 1994, p. 2328.

149 Richards & Richards, p. 649.

150 Packer, J. I. Temptation. In D.

Paul's Call to Pray

Paul was a person who prayed at all times and was consistent and continual in his prayers. He not only prayed for himself and others, he also encouraged others to pray and he led by example.

If you notice, Paul was constantly praying. We find his prayers across many of these books of the New Testament:

- Romans
- Galatians
- Ephesians
- Philippians
- Colossians
- Thessalonians
- Timothy

Prayer is not a sometime thing. It is an all the time thing. In every season it is appropriate to pray and praise God.

If you follow the example of Paul, you will see there were several key things he prayed about during his years of ministry and or asked others to pray for on his behalf. If you were wondering what to pray about or what to pray for, this list is a good starting place.

Wisdom, Knowledge & Understanding

Ephesians 1:16-17

do not cease giving thanks for you, while making mention of you in my prayers; that the God of our Lord Jesus Christ, the Father of glory, may give to you a spirit of wisdom and of revelation in the knowledge of Him.

Have you reached a point in your life whereby you have too much wisdom and knowledge? I know I have not and never will have enough wisdom and discernment. Choose to ask God daily for wisdom as you go about your life.

Living a Righteous Life

Philippians 1:9-11

And this I pray, that your love may abound still more and more in real knowledge and all discernment, so that you may approve the things that are excellent, in order to be sincere and blameless until the day of Christ; having been filled with the fruit of righteousness which comes through Jesus Christ, to the glory and praise of God.

God is always calling us to righteous living. He clearly laid this out in the 10 commandments to Moses and then Jesus refined that down to two basic precepts:

1. Love the Lord your God with all your heart, mind, body and soul.
2. Love your neighbor as yourself

By keeping it simple, Jesus is encouraging us to focus on these basic principles and understand that righteous living should not be that complicated. By living a righteous live, we can help point others to Christ and Gods Kingdom.

Sharing the Gospel

2 Thessalonians 3:1

Finally, brethren, pray for us that the word of the Lord will spread rapidly and be glorified, just as it did also with you;

It is the duty of every follower of Christ to share the Good News of the Gospel.   The Bible tells us that whoever calls upon the name of Christ will be saved.

You can choose to start preparing yourself by memorizing the Romans Road to salvation. It is a simple way to share with others the plan of salvation God has for all of us.

Romans Road

Do you know God's grace and mercy? Follow the "Romans Road" and see how God has laid out his plan of salvation for your life:

Romans 10:17

So then faith comes by hearing, and hearing by the word of God.

Romans 3:23

for all have sinned and fall short of the glory of God.

We must all realize that we are sinners and that we need forgiveness. We are not worthy of God's grace.

Romans 6:23

For the wages of sin is death, but the gift of God is eternal life in Christ Jesus our Lord.

If we remain sinners, we will die. However, if we accept Jesus as our Lord and Savior, and repent of our sins, we will have eternal life

Romans 5:8

But God demonstrates His own love toward us, in that while we were still sinners, Christ died for us.

Through Jesus, God gave us a way to be saved from our sins. God showed us His love by giving us the potential for life through the death of His Son, Jesus Christ.

Romans 10:9-10

that if you confess with your mouth the Lord Jesus and believe in your heart that God has raised Him from the dead, you will be saved. For with the heart one believes unto righteousness, and with the mouth confession is made unto salvation

Just confess that Jesus Christ is Lord and believe in your heart that God raised Him from the dead and you will be saved!

Romans 10:13

For "whoever calls on the name of the LORD shall be saved."

There are no religious formulas or rituals -- Call upon the name of the Lord and you will be saved!

God's plan of salvation is simple and free. There is nothing you can do to "earn" it. You only need to believe and confess. Do not think your sins are too great to be forgiven. Christ died for ALL sin and there is nothing so bad that you have done, that Christ cannot forgive you.

Strength & Power

Ephesians 3:14-16

For this reason I bow my knees before the Father, from whom every family in heaven and on earth derives its name, that He would grant you, according to the riches of His glory, to be strengthened with power through His Spirit in the inner man,

We can all use more strength and power in our daily walk. It is far too easy to be distracted by the cares of the world – rent/mortgage, debt, education, family, health issues, jobs, weather, wars and rumors of wars, etc. etc.

We need to remain strong in the faith and firmly focused on Christ and what He has done to transform our life and the sacrifice He made on the cross. Daily prayer and praise is a good way to stay focused.

Pray for Authorities

1 Timothy 2:1-3

First of all, then, I urge that entreaties and prayers, petitions and thanksgivings, be made on behalf of all men, for kings and all who are in authority, so that we may lead a tranquil and quiet life in all godliness and dignity. This is good and acceptable in the sight of God our Savior,

This may seem strange that Paul calls us to pray for the governing authorities (since he had been imprisoned by them and treated very poorly). In Romans 13, he more clearly calls out the need to obey the authorities. This does not mean we are called to do anything they tell us (especially if it is expressly forbidden in the Bible). Paul was wise enough to know which battles to fight and which battles to leave in the hands of God. See the verse below to better understand Paul's reasoning.

Romans 13:1-2

Every person is to be in subjection to the governing authorities. For there is no authority except from God, and those which exist are established by God. Therefore whoever resists authority has opposed the ordinance of God; and they who have opposed will receive condemnation upon themselves.

Boldness

Ephesians 6:19

and pray on my behalf, that utterance may be given to me in the opening of my mouth, to make known with boldness the mystery of the gospel,

Boldness is not reckless! It is careful consideration and thoughtful use of your time, talents and treasures to help explain the love of God to others.

Unity

Romans 15:5-6

Now may the God who gives perseverance and encouragement grant you to be of the same mind with one another according to Christ Jesus, so that with one accord you may with one voice glorify the God and Father of our Lord Jesus Christ.

Without unity, you cannot get much accomplished. Abraham Lincoln famously said – *"a house divided against itself cannot stand"*.   He was actually paraphrasing something Jesus had said in Matthew 12.

Unity in marriage, unity in the church, unity in friendship, unity in fellowship, unity of purpose!

Benjamin Franklin said at the beginning of the revolutionary war – *"we must all hang together or most assuredly we will all hang separately"*

Ecclesiastes 4:12

And if one can overpower him who is alone, two can resist him. A cord of three strands is not quickly torn apart.

Grace & Peace

1 Corinthians 1:3

Grace to you and peace from God our Father and the Lord Jesus Christ.

Peace and tranquility are two of the most precious commodities in the world.   If you have them in your home, treasure and protect them jealously.

Open Hearts

Ephesians 1:18

I pray that the eyes of your heart may be enlightened, so that you will know what is the hope of His calling, what are the riches of the glory of His inheritance in the saints,

In Proverbs we learn that we should guard our heart! Keep your heart open to God, but carefully guard it against the cares of the world.

Proverbs 4:23

Watch over your heart with all diligence, for from it flow the springs of life.

The Love of Christ

Ephesians 3:17-19

so that Christ may dwell in your hearts through faith; and that you, being rooted and grounded in love, may be able to comprehend with all the saints what is the breadth and length and height and depth, and to know the love of Christ which surpasses knowledge, that you may be filled up to all the fullness of God.

The more we try to understand the depth of the love of Christ, the more we are in awe of what He did willingly on the cross for you and for me. The love of Christ if boundless, timeless and everlasting.

Pray that you will continue to grow in your walk with Christ and know how deep his love is for you.

Knowing God's Will

Colossians 1:9

For this reason also, since the day we heard of it, we have not ceased to pray for you and to ask that you may be filled with the knowledge of His will in all spiritual wisdom and understanding,

Proverbs is a good place to go to gain wisdom and knowledge in regards to better understanding God's will and purpose of our life. Take the time to carefully study proverbs and imprint those verses on your heart and mind. Then dig deeper into the New Testament and choose to be a student of the Bible.

Daily prayer and praise will keep you grounded in your walk with Christ and will help you to better understand God's will for your life.

Growing Faith

1 Thessalonians 3:9-10
For what thanks can we render to God for you in return for all the joy with which we rejoice before our God on your account, as we night and day keep praying most earnestly that we may see your face, and may complete what is lacking in your faith?

Who among us could not use a little more faith! I know I could use more faith in my life. Walking by faith and not by sight is how we are called to live our life as followers of Christ. We learn in Hebrews that without faith it is impossible to please God!

Hebrews 11:6

And without faith it is impossible to please Him, for he who comes to God must believe that He is and that He is a rewarder of those who seek Him.

Salvation

Romans 10:1

Brethren, my heart's desire and my prayer to God for them is for their salvation.

The "them" in this case is the nation of Israel, as Paul had a special burden for the Jewish nation and their salvation. However, we also know Paul's desire was for all people to come to a saving knowledge for Jesus Christ.

Perseverance

Romans 15:30-33

Now I urge you, brethren, by our Lord Jesus Christ and by the love of the Spirit, to strive together with me in your prayers to God for me, that I may be rescued from those who are disobedient in Judea, and that my service for Jerusalem may prove acceptable to the saints; so that I may come to you in joy by the will of God and find refreshing rest in your company. Now the God of peace be with you all. Amen.

Perseverance is found all throughout the New Testament. In Romans 5 we find Paul talking about building character through trials and tribulations. He tells us that if we persevere through the trials, it will build character, which in turn will give us hope. It is in that hope that ultimately builds our faith and trust in God.

<u>Romans 5:3-5</u>

And not only this, but we also exult in our tribulations, knowing that tribulation brings about perseverance; and perseverance, proven character; and proven character, hope; and hope does not disappoint, because the love of God has been poured out within our hearts through the Holy Spirit who was given to us.

Comforting Others

<u>2 Corinthians 1:3-4</u>

Blessed be the God and Father of our Lord Jesus Christ, the Father of mercies and God of all comfort, who comforts us in all our affliction so that we will be able to comfort those who are in any affliction with the comfort with which we ourselves are comforted by God.

Did you ever wonder why you were going through a particular storm in life? Or perhaps you are in the middle of storm right now.   It has been said that we are all heading into a storm, in the middle of a storm or coming out of a storm.

Stop to consider for a moment, that God is using this storm in your life to help build your perseverance, character and hope.   Knowing that you will have the opportunity to comfort another when they are going through a similar storm and perhaps you can share the Good News of the gospel of Jesus and how He helped sustain and guide you in the storm.

Becoming more mature

<u>2 Corinthians 13:7-9</u>

Now we pray to God that you do no wrong; not that we ourselves may appear approved, but that you may do what is right, even though we may appear unapproved. For we can do nothing against the truth, but only for the truth. For we rejoice when we ourselves are weak but you are strong; this we also pray for, that you be made complete.

I am in my 50's as I write this book and in many ways still consider myself immature in so many areas of my life.   I have realized that I will never reach full maturity and knowledge of God's word while I walk on this earth. There is simply too much to comprehend.

However, that does not relieve me of the obligation to grow and gain as much maturity as possible. Is there such a thing as being to mature in the faith and knowledge of God?

Continuing a good work (finishing well)

Philippians 1:3-6

I thank my God in all my remembrance of you, always offering prayer with joy in my every prayer for you all, in view of your participation in the gospel from the first day until now. For I am confident of this very thing, that He who began a good work in you will perfect it until the day of Christ Jesus.

Finishing well! I wrote an entire book on finishing well. Continuing in a good work for God's Kingdom is an excellent way to put yourself on the road to finishing well. Remember, it is your choice as to whether or not you will finish well and continue a good work.

You may not get to choose your circumstances, but you ALWAYS get to choose your response. Consider well what you will choose.

Thankfulness

Romans 1:8

First, I thank my God through Jesus Christ for you all, because your faith is being proclaimed throughout the whole world.

1 Thessalonians 1:2

We give thanks to God always for all of you, making mention of you in our prayers;

Thankfulness is a consistent and constant theme when it comes to prayer. Paul was certainly one who was incredibly thankful not only for his salvation, but also for the work he was doing for Gods Kingdom.
Paul was thankful in spite of his circumstances. He chose to be thankful, even in prison and chains. Thankfulness is an attitude that is a reflection of trust in God.

Praying without ceasing

Ephesians 1:15-16

For this reason I too, having heard of the faith in the Lord Jesus which exists among you and your love for all the saints, 1do not cease giving thanks for you, while making mention of you in my prayers;

Colossians 1:3

We give thanks to God, the Father of our Lord Jesus Christ, praying always for you,

2 Timothy 1:3

I thank God, whom I serve with a clear conscience the way my forefathers did, as I constantly remember you in my prayers night and day,

Are you a person who is consistent and constant in their prayer life? Paul certainly was a prayer warrior.

Abounding Love

1 Thessalonians 3:11-13

Now may our God and Father Himself and Jesus our Lord direct our way to you; and may the Lord cause you to increase and abound in love for one another, and for all people, just as we also do for you; so that He may establish your hearts without blame in holiness before our God and Father at the coming of our Lord Jesus with all His saints.

1 Corinthians 13 is called the love chapter. It speaks of the excellence of love. Take the time to read these verses and contemplate how much better off we would be if we only showed just a little more love towards our fellow believers, neighbors, friends, family, strangers, and even our enemies. Read these words and mediate on the meaning of love.

1 Corinthians 13: 1-13

If I speak with the tongues of men and of angels, but do not have **love***, I have become a noisy gong or a clanging cymbal. If I have the gift of prophecy, and know all mysteries and all knowledge; and if I have all faith, so as to remove mountains, but do not have* **love***, I am nothing. And if I give all my possessions to feed the poor, and if I surrender my body to be burned, but do not have* **love***, it profits me nothing.*

Love *is patient,* **love** *is kind and is not jealous;* **love** *does not brag and is not arrogant, does not act unbecomingly; it does not seek its own, is not provoked, does not take into account a wrong suffered, does not rejoice in unrighteousness, but rejoices with the truth; bears all things, believes all things, hopes all things, endures all things.*

Love *never fails; but if there are gifts of prophecy, they will be done away; if there are tongues, they will cease; if there is knowledge, it will be done away. For we know in part and we prophesy in part; but when the perfect comes, the partial will be done away. When I was a child, I used to speak like a child, think like a child, reason like a child; when I became a man, I did away with childish things. For now we see in a mirror dimly, but then face to face; now I know in part, but then I will know fully just as I also have been fully known.*

But now faith, hope, **love***, abide these three; but the greatest of these is* **love***.*

As we close out this chapter, you can see Paul had a vigorous and thoughtful prayer life. As you consider your own prayer life, take heed to follow the example of Paul. This list would be a good starting place for your prayer life. Take the opportunity to personalize this list for yourself and your family.

- Wisdom, Knowledge & Understanding
- Living a Righteous Life
- Sharing the Gospel
- Strength & Power
- Pray for Authorities
- Boldness
- Unity
- Grace & Peace
- Open Hearts
- The Love of Christ
- Knowing God's Will
- Growing Faith
- Salvation
- Perseverance
- Comforting Others
- Becoming more mature
- Continuing a good work (finishing well)
- Thankfulness
- Praying without ceasing
- Abounding Love

Famous Prayers

Here are some of the more famous prayers from the Bible as well as from other individuals. Some of these you might recognize and others may be new to you, but know that all of them are prayers to our God.

Psalm 23

The Lord is my shepherd,
I shall not want.
He makes me lie down in green pastures;
He leads me beside quiet waters.
He restores my soul;
He guides me in the paths of righteousness
For His name's sake.
Even though I walk through the valley of the shadow of death,
I fear no evil, for You are with me;
Your rod and Your staff, they comfort me.
You prepare a table before me in the presence of my enemies;
You have anointed my head with oil;
My cup overflows.
Surely goodness and lovingkindness will follow me all the days of my life,
And I will dwell in the house of the Lord forever.

Numbers 6:24-26

The Lord bless you, and keep you;
The Lord make His face shine on you,
And be gracious to you;
The Lord lift up His countenance on you,
And give you peace.'

Matthew 6:9-13) – The Lord's Prayer

"Pray, then, in this way:

'Our Father who is in heaven,
Hallowed be Your name.
'Your kingdom come.
Your will be done,
On earth as it is in heaven.
'Give us this day [a]our daily bread.
'And forgive us our debts, as we also have forgiven our debtors.
'And do not lead us into temptation, but deliver us from evil.
For Yours is the kingdom and the power and the glory forever. Amen.

Prayer for Peace
Lead me from Death to Life,
from Falsehood to Truth,
Lead me from Despair to Hope,
from Fear to Trust,
Lead me from Hate to Love,
from War to Peace,
Let Peace fill our Heart,
our World, our Universe.
Amen.

The Serenity Prayer
God grant me the serenity
to accept the things I cannot change,
Courage to change the things I can,
And wisdom to know the difference.
Amen. - Reinhold Neibuhr

The Serenity Prayer (long version)

God grant me the serenity
to accept the things I cannot change,
Courage to change the things I can,
And wisdom to know the difference.
Living one day at a time;
enjoying one moment at a time;
accepting hardships as the pathway to peace;
taking, as He did,
this sinful world as it is,
not as I would have it:
Trusting that He will make all things
right if I surrender to His Will;
that I may be reasonably happy in this life
and supremely happy with Him forever in the next. Amen.
-Reinhold Neibuhr

Prayer of Saint Francis

Lord, make me an instrument of your peace;
where there is hatred, let me sow love,
where there is injury, pardon,
where there is doubt, faith,
where there is despair, hope,
where there is darkness, light,
and where there is sadness, joy.
O Divine Master,
grant that I may not so much seek
to be consoled as to console,
to be understood as to understand,
to be loved as to love.
For it is in giving that we receive,
it is in pardoning that we are pardoned,
and it is in dying that we are born to eternal life.
Amen.

An Evening Prayer

O Lord my God,
thank you for bringing this day to a close.
Thank you for giving me rest
in body and soul.
Your hand has been over me
and has guarded and preserved me.
Forgive my lack of faith
and any wrong that I have done today,
and help me to forgive all who have wronged us.
Let me sleep in peace under your protection,
and keep me from all the temptations of darkness.
Into your hands I commend my loved ones.
I commend to you my body and soul.
O God, your holy name be praised.
Amen.
-Dietrich Bonhoeffer

Prayer of St. Richard of Chichester

Thanks be to thee, my Lord Jesus Christ,
For all the benefits thou hast won for me,
For all the pains and insults thou hast borne for me.
O most merciful Redeemer, Friend, and Brother,
May I know thee more clearly,
Love thee more dearly,
And follow thee more nearly:
For ever and ever.
Amen.

The Irish Blessing

May the road rise to meet you,
May the wind be always at your back,
May the sun shine warm upon your face,
The rains fall soft upon your fields and,
Until we meet again,
May God hold you in the palm of His hand.

--- Anonymous

Make Me an Instrument of Your Peace

Lord, make me an instrument of your peace.
Where there is hatred, let me sow love,
Where there is injury, pardon
Where there is doubt, faith,
Where there is despair, hope,
Where there is darkness, light,
Where there is sadness, joy.
O Divine Master, grant that I may not so much
seek to be consoled as to console,
not so much to be understood as to understand,
not so much to be loved, as to love;
for it is in giving that we receive,
it is in pardoning that we are pardoned,
it is in dying that we awake to eternal life.

--- St. Francis of Assisi

Christ Be With Me

Christ with me, Christ before me, Christ behind me,
Christ in me, Christ beneath me, Christ above me,
Christ on my right, Christ on my left,
Christ where I lie, Christ where I sit, Christ where I arise,
Christ in the heart of everyone who thinks of me,
Christ in the mouth of every one who speaks to me,
Christ in every eye that sees me,
Christ in every ear that hears me.
Salvation is of the Lord.
Salvation is of the Christ.
May your salvation, Lord, be ever with us.
--- St. Patrick

Dearest Lord, teach me to be generous;
Teach me to serve thee as thou deservest;
To give and not to count the cost,
To fight and not to seek for rest,
To labour and not to seek reward,
Save that of knowing that I do thy will.
-Ignatius of Loyola

Prayer by the Numbers

I have always been fascinated with facts and statistics, so I hope this section does not put you to sleep, but rather I hope it helps to give you a better feel for how prayer is represented in the Bible.   These are fun facts I found while doing research for this book.

9 – Types of prayer found in the Bible

25 – Number of times Jesus is found praying

41 – Number of times Paul mentions prayer and praying

100-300+ - Number of times the word pray is mentioned in the Bible (varies by translation)

450 – Number of answered prayers in the Bible

650 – Approximate number of prayers in the Bible

Source: thegospelcoalition.org/ May 5, 2014

Prayer Quotes

"Prayer is a shield to the soul, a sacrifice to God, and a scourge for Satan".
John Bunyan

"More things are wrought by prayer than this world dreams of."
Alfred Lord Tennyson

"The fewer the words the better prayer." Martin Luther

"True prayer is neither a mere mental exercise nor a vocal performance. It
is far deeper than that - it is spiritual transaction with the Creator of
Heaven and Earth." - Charles Spurgeon

"Prayer does not fit us for the greater work; prayer is the greater work."
Oswald Chambers

"Prayer is an effort of will." Oswald Chambers

"Pray as if everything depended on God, and work as if everything
depended upon man." Francis J. Spellman

"God does nothing but by prayer, and everything with it."
John Wesley

"Our prayer and God's mercy are like two buckets in a well; while one
ascends, the other descends." Arthur Hopkins

"It is because of the hasty and superficial conversation with God that the
sense of sin is so weak and that no motives have power to help you to hate
and flee from sin as you should." A.W. Tozer

"Every great movement of God can be traced to a kneeling figure."
D. L. Moody

"Don't pray when you feel like it. Have an appointment with the Lord and keep it. A man is powerful on his knees." Corrie Ten Boom

"Is prayer your steering wheel or your spare tire?" - Corrie ten Boom

"Any concern too small to be turned into a prayer is too small to be made into a burden." - Corrie Ten Boom

"Work as if you were to live a hundred years. Pray as if you were to die tomorrow." Benjamin Franklin

"Prayer is the acid test of devotion." ~ Samuel Chadwick

"Prayer requires more of the heart than the tongue."
Adam Clarke

"If you believe in prayer at all, expect God to hear you. If you do not expect, you will not have. God will not hear you unless you believe He will hear you; but if you believe He will, He will be as good as your faith." - Charles Spurgeon

"Prayer – secret, fervent, believing prayer – lies at the root of all personal godliness.+ Williams Carey

"There are parts of our calling, works of the Holy Spirit, and defeats of the darkness that will come no other way than through furious, fervent, faith-filled, unceasing prayer." - Beth Moore

"To get nations back on their feet, we must first get down on our knees." - Billy Graham

"The prayer offered to God in the morning during your quiet time is the key that unlocks the door of the day. Any athlete knows that it is the start that ensures a good finish." - Adrian Rogers

"Prayer is not monologue, but dialogue. Gods voice in response to mine is its most essential part". Andrew Murray

Jesus as the example

Jesus as the example

In Matthew 26, we find the story of Jesus praying in the garden of Gethsemane. Jesus has just finished the last supper with all of his disciples and it was his last opportunity to pour into them and fellowship with them before his trial and crucifixion. Jesus knows the physical pain that is coming and the ultimate separation from the Father as he dies for the sins of the world. So where do his thoughts turn? They turn to prayer.

Jesus was clearly distressed as he knew what was coming. In verse 37-38 the Bible says he was "grieved and distressed". He went deeper into the garden and took his three closest disciples with him (Peter, James and John) and asked them to stay with him while he prayed. He even said this to them: "My soul is deeply grieved, to the point of death; remain here and keep watch with Me."

You see even our Lord and Savior knew that in time of trouble, the first thing to do was to pray to the Father. In addition, we also see that in this time of distress Jesus wanted to keep close fellowship with his disciples not only to continue to teach them, but also to have them as prayer partners and to help encourage Him.

Finally we see in Jesus's prayer that he shows the **highest form of worship** to God our Father. He asks for the "cup" to pass from him, but then he say "not my will, but your will be done". God is looking for all of us to be obedient to His call in our life. Here Jesus knows what is coming and yet surrenders his own will to that of the Father. You see, obedience is the highest form of worship we can give back to God.

It is a great example of us to know that in our times of trouble we should first turn to the Father in prayer and lift our voice to Him and continue in fellowship with other believers so that we will be encouraged and can even encourage others. Finally we know we can and should praise and worship God no matter the circumstances in our life.

The Garden of Gethsemane

Matthew 26:36-46

Then Jesus came with them to a place called Gethsemane, and said to His disciples, "Sit here while I go over there and pray."

And He took with Him Peter and the two sons of Zebedee, and began to be grieved and distressed. Then He said to them, "My soul is deeply grieved, to the point of death; remain here and keep watch with Me."

And He went a little beyond them, and fell on His face and prayed, saying, "My Father, if it is possible, let this cup pass from Me; yet not as I will, but as You will."

And He came to the disciples and found them sleeping, and said to Peter, "So, you men could not keep watch with Me for one hour? Keep watching and praying that you may not enter into temptation; the spirit is willing, but the flesh is weak."

He went away again a second time and prayed, saying, "My Father, if this cannot pass away unless I drink it, Your will be done."
Again He came and found them sleeping, for their eyes were heavy. And He left them again, and went away and prayed a third time, saying the same thing once more.

Then He came to the disciples and said to them, "Are you still sleeping and resting? Behold, the hour is at hand and the Son of Man is being betrayed into the hands of sinners. Get up, let us be going; behold, the one who betrays Me is at hand!"

Finally, consider Jesus attitude and actions as he faces this situation. His attitude is one of love for the world and for His creation. His actions are those of obedience to the Father. He does not pray one time in this scene, he prays three times to the Father. Jesus is and continues to be the perfect model for our lives and how we should ultimately face the trials, trouble and tribulations that **WILL** come in our lifetime.

High Priestly Prayer

In John 17 we find the entire chapter is Jesus praying what has been called the High Priestly Prayer. There are three distinct phases of the prayer.

Phase 1 - verses 1-5 he is praying for Himself
Phase 2 – verses 6-19 he prays for his disciples
Phase 3 – verses 20 -26 he prays for future believers

Take the time to read and meditate on this entire chapter as you consider how much Jesus chooses to pray.

Choosing the 12 Apostles

Luke 6:12-13

It was at this time that He went off to the mountain to pray, and He spent the whole night in prayer to God. And when day came, He called His disciples to Him and chose twelve of them, whom He also named as apostles:

Before making an important decision about the men who would carry on with God's Kingdom work when He was gone, Jesus spent the entire night in prayer. When it comes to leadership it is critical to have the right team in place. People you can trust and who you know will fully implement your wishes and desires. Jesus also know how much these men would suffer for sharing the Gospel and you can only imagine how he was praying for their faith, boldness, protection and strength.

Before Feeding 5,000 & 4,000

Luke 9:16

Then He took the five loaves and the two fish, and looking up to heaven, He blessed them, and broke them, and kept giving them to the disciples to set before the people.

Matthew 15:36

and He took the seven loaves and the fish; and giving thanks, He broke them and started giving them to the disciples, and the disciples gave them to the people.

This would be a miracle performed before thousands of people and Jesus wanted to make sure his disciples understood that God should receive the honor and glory. He offered blessing and thanks for the food they received. It is also important to note that while Jesus is certainly concerned about the condition of their hearts and minds, He also understood they had basic physical needs that needed to be met. Certainly people are much more willing to listen to the message if their stomach is not growling!

When He was Baptized

Luke 3:21-22

Now when all the people were baptized, Jesus was also baptized, and while He was praying, heaven was opened, and the Holy Spirit descended upon Him in bodily form like a dove, and a voice came out of heaven, "You are My beloved Son, in You I am well-pleased."

John the Baptist was the cousin of Jesus and he was the forerunner of the Lord. As Jesus prepared to begin his earthly ministry, He started with the act that would foreshadow his death, burial and resurrection. He was also setting an example not only for his disciples but for all of us who would choose to follow him and call ourselves Christians.

While baptism is not necessary for salvation, it is a very important public act of acknowledgement of a changed life and choice to follow Christ as your Lord and Savior.

When Lazarus was raised from the dead

<u>John 11:41-42</u>

So they removed the stone. Then Jesus raised His eyes, and said, "Father, I thank You that You have heard Me. I knew that You always hear Me; but because of the people standing around I said it, so that they may believe that You sent Me."

One of the more famous verses in the Bible is very short – Jesus wept.

This verse is recorded after Jesus saw the sorrow of Lazarus's family and his own sorrow as well.

Jesus offers this very public and vocal prayer to build the faith of those around Him and to also give glory and honor to God for what was about to be done.   Jesus knew this would be a powerful miracle that would be repeatedly told throughout the ages and it was important that those around Him knew this was a miracle of God.

On the Cross

Isn't it amazing that even on the cross, bearing the sins of the whole world on his shoulders, He would offer prayers to God at the most destitute of times.

In the one prayer his is asking for forgiveness of the ignorance of those persecuting Him and in the other prayer he is showing how much faith and trust he had in God.   Jesus shows us that prayer is appropriate and needed in at all times, not only for ourselves, but for others as well. You may be facing a terrible trial and yet you could take time to try to think of others and pray for them.

<u>Luke 23:34</u>

But Jesus was saying, "Father, forgive them; for they do not know what they are doing." And they cast lots, dividing up His garments among themselves.

<u>Luke 23:46</u>

And Jesus, crying out with a loud voice, said, "Father, into Your hands I commit My spirit." Having said this, He breathed His last.

Jesus as our advocate

I love these verses below. Just think about it, Jesus is sitting at the right hand of the Father continually making intercession for us. He is always there, he never sleeps, never falters, never gives up. Morning, noon and night we have Jesus as our advocate. How very thankful we should be for a wonderful Savior!

1 John 2:1

My little children, I am writing these things to you so that you may not sin. And if anyone sins, we have an Advocate with the Father, Jesus Christ the righteous;

Romans 8:34

who is the one who condemns? Christ Jesus is He who died, yes, rather who was raised, who is at the right hand of God, who also intercedes for us.

Hebrews 7:25

Therefore He is able also to save forever those who draw near to God through Him, since He always lives to make intercession for them.

Where Jesus Prayed

I think it is interesting to note the different places Jesus prayed. Certainly being outside surrounded by nature and seeing God's glory everywhere would be an excellent place to have solitude and communion with God in prayer.

Riverside – when He was baptized
Mountaintop – before big decision
Wilderness – after healing and ministering
Deserted place – before he preached
Outside a tomb – Raise Lazarus
Upper Room – Last Supper
Garden – Before he was betrayed
Hilltop – on the Cross

The Perfect Prayer

Many people, who are not students of the Bible, know the "Lord's Prayer". Many have been taught this as young children and remember the words they have memorized.

In our family, we pray this prayer each night as a family as a benediction to close out our family prayer time.   It is a great way for us to end each and every day.

Matthew 6:6- 9-13

But you, when you pray, go into your inner room, close your door and pray to your Father who is in secret, and your Father who sees what is done in secret will reward you.......

"Pray, then, in this way:
'Our Father who is in heaven,
Hallowed be Your name.
'Your kingdom come.
Your will be done,
On earth as it is in heaven.
'Give us this day our daily bread.
'And forgive us our debts, as we also have forgiven our debtors.
'And do not lead us into temptation, but deliver us from evil. For Yours is the kingdom and the power and the glory forever. Amen.'

In context, Jesus was teaching the Sermon on the Mount. This is where he laid out many of the basic principles of living a Godly life and even offered direct contradiction to what the world was teaching. Here are the subjects he taught that day:

- The Beatitudes
- Salt & Light
- How to handle anger
- Lust
- Divorce
- Vows
- Retaliation
- Loving your enemies
- Giving to the needy
- **Prayer**
- Fasting
- Money
- Worry
- Asking, Seeking & Knocking
- The way to heaven
- Bearing fruit
- House built on rock and sand

As you can see, prayer was only one aspect of what Jesus taught that day on the mount. Note that it came almost in the middle of what He was teaching. Study Matthew chapters 5-8 to better understand the entire Sermon on the Mount. There is more than enough material there to keep you busy for weeks on end.

The reason some have called this the perfect prayer is because in a succinct passage we find the key elements of the Christian faith.

In the first part of the prayer we find three petitions that focus on God:

- Acknowledgment of God as our heavenly father
- Adoration and Praise for the holiness of God
- Acceptance of His will and way – He is in control

In the last part of the prayer we find the focus on our need for God's help:

- Give – meet our physical needs
- Forgive – meet our spiritual and relational needs
- Deliver – protect us

If you recall from the earlier chapter on A-C-T-S praying, this suggested a systematic approach to prayer – Adoration, Confession, Thanksgiving, and Supplication. What we find in the Lord's Prayer is a similar model for this type of praying. While it does not follow the exact pattern of A-C-T-S praying, all of the elements are there.

In the first part of the prayer we can see the adoration and praise to God and recognition of who He is. In the next section we see the confession and asking for forgiveness and the final part contains the supplication about not being led into temptation and delivery from evil. Now you may ask – where is the thanksgiving? Remember that thanksgiving is the attitude in which we pray. Therefore, the underlying attitude of this entire prayer is one of thanksgiving.

Ultimately, the key to this prayer is that it was Jesus himself who taught this prayer. If our Lord thought it so important to teach this lesson then perhaps it is we who should take it to heart and make it a part of our prayer life. I particularly love the shortness and simplicity of this prayer. Jesus always had a way of making the complicated uncomplicated.

When you think about it, Jesus was asked about which was the greatest commandment. He then went on to boil down the 10 commandants to two key principles:

- Love and Worship God
- Love you Neighbor

Matthew 22:36-40

"Teacher, which is the great commandment in the Law?" And He said to him, "'You shall love the Lord your God with all your heart, and with all your soul, and with all your mind.' This is the great and foremost commandment. The second is like it, 'You shall love your neighbor as yourself.' On these two commandments depend the whole Law and the Prophets."

In other words, keep it simple. God is not looking for complicated prayer. He is looking for a relationship!

How Not to Pray

There is a wrong way to pray and the Bible clearly lays out the parameters for poor prayer. Below is a list of wrong ways to approach God in prayer.

1. Praying with wrong motives
2. Praying with meaningless repetition
3. Praying with a prideful perspective
4. Praying with no intention of turning from your sin
5. For Appearance's Sake
6. Being an Evil Doers

Wrong Motives

James 4:3

You ask and do not receive, because you ask with wrong motives, so that you may spend it on your pleasures.

In case you did not know, God is Omniscient, Omni-Present and Omnipotent – in other words, God is All Knowing, Always Present and All Powerful. Therefore, if we think we can approach the King of Glory with wrong motives and "fool" God, then we are only fooling ourselves. God knows the deepest desires of our hearts and minds and he weights and knows our motives.

Meaningless Repetition

<u>Matthew 6:7-8</u>

"And when you are praying, do not use meaningless repetition as the Gentiles do, for they suppose that they will be heard for their many words. So do not be like them; for your Father knows what you need before you ask Him.

In the same way, praying with meaningless repetition is also a non-starter with God. He is looking for meaningful and thoughtful prayers. Sometimes we think more words are better and yet the Bible tells us when we do not know what to pray, then the Holy Spirit will actually help us in our weakness and make intercession for us with groaning too deep for words.

<u>Romans 8:26</u>

In the same way the Spirit also helps our weakness; for we do not know how to pray as we should, but the Spirit Himself intercedes for us with groaning too deep for words;

Talk to God just as you would talk to your own father. You would not go to your own father with meaningless bather! You would talk to him with words of reason and meaning.   You would bring you cares and troubles to him. You would want to share your deepest concerns, hurt and emotions. God is there to listen and hear your prayers.

Pride

<u>Luke 18:9-14</u>

And He also told this parable to some people who trusted in themselves that they were righteous, and viewed others with contempt: "Two men went up into the temple to pray, one a Pharisee and the other a tax collector. The Pharisee stood and was praying this to himself: 'God, I thank You that I am not like other people: swindlers, unjust, adulterers, or even like this tax collector. I fast twice a week; I pay tithes of all that I get.' But the tax collector, standing some distance away, was even unwilling to lift up his eyes to heaven, but was beating his breast, saying, 'God, be merciful to me, the sinner!' I tell you, this man went to his house justified rather than the other; for everyone who exalts himself will be humbled, but he who humbles himself will be exalted."

God has no use for the prideful! He is looking for us to enter his courtyards with humility and knowledge that we are not worthy of His grace and forgiveness. God does not want us to compare ourselves to other people. That is the wrong measuring stick to use. We can only measure ourselves against Christ and his goodness and mercy and know we will come up short of perfection, but through His shed blood on the cross we are made worthy.

Unrepentant Sin

Proverbs 28:9

He who turns away his ear from listening to the law,
Even his prayer is an abomination.

The Bible tells us in the verse above that God is not going to listen to or hear our prayers if we have no intention of turning from our sin. God is always ready, willing and able to listen to our prayers and forgive us our sins, but He closes his ears to our prayers when He knows the intentions of our hearts and our unwillingness to truly turn away from our sin.

For Appearance's Sake

Mark 12:38-40

In His teaching He was saying: "Beware of the scribes who like to walk around in long robes, and like respectful greetings in the market places, and chief seats in the synagogues and places of honor at banquets, who devour widows' houses, and for appearance's sake offer long prayers; these will receive greater condemnation."

We have all heard those long prayers from people who are talking not to God, but to those who are gathered around. They drone on and on and on hoping to impress the people and only annoying God. They are only worried about how they will appear before their fellow man, instead of truly lifting a prayer to God. Remember, it is not the number of words or the type of words, rather it is the intent of the heart.

Evil Doers

1 Peter 3:12

"For the eyes of the Lord are toward the righteous,
And His ears attend to their prayer,
But the face of the Lord is against those who do evil."

Because God is Holy (Isaiah 6:3… Holy, Holy, Holy is the Lord of Hosts), He cannot and will not stand for evil or those who do evil.   Our righteousness through Christ is what allows us to seek God's face and bring our prayers and petitions to Him.   Put away your evil thoughts and desires and turn from your wickedness and God will hear your prayers.

Asking!

We have covered many of these verses in this book, but I wanted to bring them all together in one place. As you consider how to get answers to your prayers, then follow the guidance of these verses below. To be clear, I do not offer this as some magical panacea for God's perfect will in our life nor am I am advocating the "prosperity gospel of name it and claim it"

I only point out clear direction given to us in the Bible in how we should pray and expect an answer. Remember God always has our best interest in mind, so sometimes the answer will be a resounding NO (or even a quiet NO).

I have had a number of clear instances in my life where I specifically prayed for opportunities and the doors were closed. At the time I did not understand or clearly comprehend what God was doing when He said NO! I admit to being hurt and even angry in my immature faith and walk at the time.

I remember specifically praying about a job opportunity that I just knew was perfect for me and my family. I was the perfect candidate with the right skills and knowledge. It would have been a nice promotion and not even required a relocation or move. I just knew this was an open door.

My Bride and I earnestly prayed for the new job. I got the initial interview, the follow up interview and even made the final list of candidates. I just knew the job was mine.

However, God had another plan. I got a call a few days later that the job had been filled by another person and I just could not understand why this seemingly open door was slammed in my face.

Well, they say hindsight is 20/20 and as Paul Harvey used to say, now I can tell you the rest of the story.

Six months after I missed out on that particular job, the company went through a reorganization and that entire department was let go! Nobody in the group survived the job cuts! However, I was safely ensconced in my current job and our group was untouched by the restructure.

Looking back, I can see how God had my best interests in mind all along! He knew what was coming and I was saved from a "sure thing". From this experience I have learned to walk more closely with God and trust and have faith that He has my back.

One other thought for those of you who are married.

If you are praying and asking, make sure you and your spouse are firmly and completely aligned on the "ASK". I have learned in my own marriage that God will speak to both of us and give us both clear direction. If we do not both get clear direction, then we turn away from any opportunity, no matter how lucrative or fruitful.

I had another job opportunity that seemed completely God ordained! It would have been incredibly impactful financially, professionally and personally. The stars seemed to be aligned and God seemed to be opening the door. Both my Bride and I were initially aligned on the opportunity as it was presented and we prayed about it. However, it was a very long process over many months before an offer was finally made.

We finally got the job offer and my Bride told me after much prayer and reflection she had no peace about the job. She initially did not want to share this with me, because she knew I would be disappointed. I could not believe it! I thought the door was wide open. It seemed like a slam dunk. I was a bit frustrated, but was also wise enough to trust that God would have to give both of us a peace and direction for this job.

I felt a bit foolish when I had to call the company and turn down the offer. They could not understand and I could not clearly articulate our decision (it is hard to tell a company that you prayed about it and then had no peace – they think you are crazy). From a worldly point of view, it made no sense at all!

To make a long story short, it was the right decision. My Bride did not feel comfortable with the move, because it would have taken us away from our adult children and she just sensed we would be needed. She was right! About six months later we were faced with an epic family crisis that required all of our energy and attention. If we had taken the new job in a new state the consequences to our family could have been devastating.

As it was, we were here and able to work through the trials and storms. This event further strengthened my faith and trust in God when the answer was NO or when my Bride and I were not aligned.

So as you consider bringing your prayers and petitions to God, do not be surprised when He answers some with YES and do not be surprised when He answers others with NO. In either case be sure to offer praise and honor to God.

Remember He is a good Father who wants to give his children the desires of their heart! He is good all the time.

Verses on Asking

As you read these different verses on asking God in prayer, consider the words used to describe how the believer should bring these petitions before The King.

- Consider the Will of God
- Ask in Confidence
- Ask with Thanksgiving
- Ask with Belief
- Abide in God
- Ask in Faith
- Ask in Forgiveness
- Be Fruitful

Philippians 4:6

Be anxious for nothing, but in everything by prayer and supplication with thanksgiving let your requests be made known to God.

John 16:24
Until now you have asked for nothing in My name; ask and you will receive, so that your joy may be made full.

Mark 11:24
Therefore I say to you, all things for which you pray and ask, believe that you have received them, and they will be granted you.

1 John 5:14-15
This is the confidence which we have before Him, that, if we ask anything according to His will, He hears us. And if we know that He hears us in whatever we ask, we know that we have the requests which we have asked from Him.

Matthew 21:22
And all things you ask in prayer, believing, you will receive."

John 15:7

If you abide in Me, and My words abide in you, ask whatever you wish, and it will be done for you.

James 1:6-7

But he must ask in faith without any doubting, for the one who doubts is like the surf of the sea, driven and tossed by the wind. For that man ought not to expect that he will receive anything from the Lord,

Matthew 7:7

"Ask, and it will be given to you; seek, and you will find; knock, and it will be opened to you.

1 John 5:14

This is the confidence which we have before Him, that, if we ask anything according to His will, He hears us.

John 15:16

You did not choose Me but I chose you, and appointed you that you would go and bear fruit, and that your fruit would remain, so that whatever you ask of the Father in My name He may give to you.

Mark 11:23-25

Truly I say to you, whoever says to this mountain, 'Be taken up and cast into the sea,' and does not doubt in his heart, but believes that what he says is going to happen, it will be granted him. Therefore I say to you, all things for which you pray and ask, believe that you have received them, and they will be granted you. Whenever you stand praying, forgive, if you have anything against anyone, so that your Father who is in heaven will also forgive you your transgressions.

John 14:13-14

Whatever you ask in My name, that will I do, so that the Father may be glorified in the Son. If you ask Me anything in My name, I will do it.

Warning about asking

Below are some clear warnings when you do ask! You can fool other people, but you can never fool nor can you hide from God. He knows your heart even better than you know your heart. If your heart and motives are wrong, God will not consider your prayers.

James 4:3

You ask and do not receive, because you ask with wrong motives, so that you may spend it on your pleasures.

Hebrews 11:6

And without faith it is impossible to please Him, for he who comes to God must believe that He is and that He is a rewarder of those who seek Him.

Psalm 66:18-20

If I regard wickedness in my heart,
The Lord will not hear;
But certainly God has heard;
He has given heed to the voice of my prayer.
Blessed be God,
Who has not turned away my prayer
Nor His lovingkindness from me.

Fasting

In the Bible, we find fasting and prayer interlinked on many occasions. Fasting is a voluntary act whereby a person will forgo food for a period of time so they can concentrate their entire being to prayer and seeking God. Temporary fasting will bring about hunger pangs from the body, which will prompt you to pray and focus on your relationship with God.

Fasting is never to be done so that others can know you are fasting. It is done in secret as an act of worship and fellowship with God.   Fasting should be about bringing honor and glory to God!

Jesus taught the lesson of fasting as part of his message on the Sermon on the Mount.

Matthew 6:17-18

But you, when you fast, anoint your head and wash your face so that your fasting will not be noticed by men, but by your Father who is in secret; and your Father who sees what is done in secret will reward you.

There was a time not long ago when my beautiful Bride went on a week-long fast and none of us knew it! She never mentioned it and she was her usually perky self all week long.   It was only later that I found out she had been fasting and praying.   I praise God for a Bride who is willing to go the extra mile to pray and fast for her family and do so with a great attitude and humility.

We have many examples of fasting in the Bible in both the Old Testament and the New Testament.   There were many different reasons given for fasting and praying; whether to prepare for an important decision, seeking wisdom, protection, safety, or in sorrow, the point of the fasting was to worship and draw closer to God.   One thing is clear, fasting is not about us! It is all about God!

Safety and Protection

In the book of Ezra we find fasting and praying as they prepare for a long journey.

Ezra 8:21-23

Then I proclaimed a fast there at the river of Ahava, that we might humble ourselves before our God to seek from Him a safe journey for us, our little ones, and all our possessions. For I was ashamed to request from the king troops and horsemen to protect us from the enemy on the way, because we had said to the king, "The hand of our God is favorably disposed to all those who seek Him, but His power and His anger are against all those who forsake Him." So we fasted and sought our God concerning this matter, and He listened to our entreaty.

Mourning (sorrow & grief)

In the very beginning of the book of Nehemiah, we find Nehemiah getting news that the holy city of Jerusalem has been in disrepair and that the walls are crumbling and the gate have been burned. There is no longer any protection for the city and Nehemiah is devastated by the news. We also find in 2 Samuel, David and the nation of Israel mourning when Saul and Jonathan are killed.

Nehemiah 1:1-4

The words of Nehemiah the son of Hacaliah.
Now it happened in the month Chislev, in the twentieth year, while I was in Susa the capitol, that Hanani, one of my brothers, and some men from Judah came; and I asked them concerning the Jews who had escaped and had survived the captivity, and about Jerusalem. They said to me, "The remnant there in the province who survived the captivity are in great distress and reproach, and the wall of Jerusalem is broken down and its gates are burned with fire." When I heard these words, I sat down and wept and mourned for days; and I was fasting and praying before the God of heaven.

2 Samuel 1:12

They mourned and wept and fasted until evening for Saul and his son Jonathan and for the people of the Lord and the house of Israel, because they had fallen by the sword.

Appointing Leaders

In the book of Acts, we find Paul and Barnabas looking for elders and leaders to continue the work they had started.

Acts 14:23

When they had appointed elders for them in every church, having prayed with fasting, they commended them to the Lord in whom they had believed.

Serving & Worship

Jesus has been brought to the Temple by his parents after he had been circumcised and given his name. They wanted to worship God and offer a sacrifice. They were met by two different people at the Temple that day who spoke into their life in a positive way. First Simeon blessed them and then they encountered Anna.

Luke 2:36-38

And there was a prophetess, Anna the daughter of Phanuel, of the tribe of Asher. She was advanced in years and had lived with her husband seven years after her marriage, and then as a widow to the age of eighty-four. She never left the temple, serving night and day with fastings and prayers. At that very moment she came up and began giving thanks to God, and continued to speak of Him to all those who were looking for the redemption of Jerusalem.

Deliverance and Victory

In chapter 20 of the book of Judges we find a civil war raging and the sons Israel lose 38,000 men in battle. They are desperate for deliverance and seek God through fasting and prayer and God gives them the victory.

Judges 20:26

Then all the sons of Israel and all the people went up and came to Bethel and wept; thus they remained there before the Lord and fasted that day until evening. And they offered burnt offerings and peace offerings before the Lord.

Repentance

We all know the story of Johan and the whale. What we tend to forget is the rest of the story. In Jonah chapter 3, we find him in the city of Nineveh proclaiming the word of God and the inevitable destruction because of their wickedness. However, an amazing thing happens. The people believe in God and turn from the wicked ways and God spares the city. It is a beautiful story of true repentance and deliverance.

Jonah 3:5

Then the people of Nineveh believed in God; and they called a fast and put on sackcloth from the greatest to the least of them.

Preparation

Jesus has just been baptized by his cousin John and He is about to start his earthly ministry.   Before he starts his ministry, he heads into the wilderness where he fasts for 40 days.

Luke 4:1-4

Jesus, full of the Holy Spirit, returned from the Jordan and was led around by the Spirit in the wilderness for forty days, being tempted by the devil. And He ate nothing during those days, and when they had ended, He became hungry. And the devil said to Him, "If You are the Son of God, tell this stone to become bread." And Jesus answered him, "It is written, 'Man shall not live on bread alone.'"

A Covenant

Before Jesus spent 40 days fasting, we find Moses doing the same thing in the presence of God. It was on Mount Sinai, where Moses spent time with God and received His covenant which was the Ten Commandments.

Exodus 34:28

So he was there with the Lord forty days and forty nights; he did not eat bread or drink water. And he wrote on the tablets the words of the covenant, the Ten Commandments.

Seeking Help

In 2 Chronicles, we find the leader Jehoshaphat is fearful when he finds a great multitude has invaded his country. Knowing he cannot defeat this enemy himself, he turns to God in this time of great trouble.

2 Chronicles 20:3-4

Jehoshaphat was afraid and turned his attention to seek the Lord, and proclaimed a fast throughout all Judah. So Judah gathered together to seek help from the Lord; they even came from all the cities of Judah to seek the Lord.

Righting a Wrong

In Daniel 6, we find a jealous group of busybodies who are not happy about having Daniel around the king. Therefore they devise a trap and the king steps right into their plan to destroy Daniel. The king is trapped by his own words of condemnation, but he knows Daniel is innocent and he want to right a wrong. After Daniel is thrown into the lion's den, we see the true character of the king.

Daniel 6:18

Then the king went off to his palace and spent the night fasting, and no entertainment was brought before him; and his sleep fled from him.

Ministry

In Acts chapter 13 we find men in prayer and fasting as they seek God and His will and way. In the midst of fasting, they are called to set apart Paul and Barnabas to go on the first mission trip.

Acts 13:2-3

While they were ministering to the Lord and fasting, the Holy Spirit said, "Set apart for Me Barnabas and Saul for the work to which I have called them." Then, when they had fasted and prayed and laid their hands on them, they sent them away.

Guide to Fasting

There is an excellent guide on fasting written by Dr. Bill Bright (who founded Campus Crusade for Christ) that is quite practical and useful. It is called *"The Personal Guide to Fasting and Praying"*. It includes 11 steps on how to fast and pray. He includes everything from how to start the fast, length, safety, and so much more. Also in the guide he gives seven great reasons for fasting:

- Fasting was an expected practice in both the Old and New Testament eras. For example, Moses fasted at least two recorded forty-day periods. Jesus fasted 40 days and reminded His followers to fast, "when you fast," not if you fast.
- Fasting and prayer can restore the loss of your "first love" for the Lord and result in a more intimate relationship with Christ.
- Fasting is a biblical way to truly humble yourself in the sight of God (Psalm 35:13; Ezra 8:21). King David said, "I humble myself through fasting."
- Fasting enables the Holy Spirit to reveal your true spiritual condition, resulting in brokenness, repentance and a transformed life.
- The Holy Spirit will imprint God's Word deeper on your heart, and His truth will become more meaningful to you.
- Fasting can transform your prayer life into a richer and more personal experience.
- Fasting can result in a dynamic personal revival and make you a channel of life change to others.

If you are considering a fast, then I encourage you to read and review this guide. You can find the guide at **www.CRU.org**.

https://www.cru.org/us/en/train-and-grow/spiritual-growth/fasting/personal-guide-to-fasting.html

Praying for Church Leaders and Missionaries

While it is vitally important to pray for your family and friends, it is just as important to pray for your church leaders (Preacher, Pastor, etc.) and missionaries. They are on the front lines of ministry each and every day. They are doing battle with internal enemies (those who cause strife and bitterness in the church) as well as doing battle with external enemies (local community, Satan, governments, and others). They also are called upon to minister to the needs of the hurting and needy as well as shepherding their own flock.

These ministers of the Gospel not only need our prayers, but they deserve our prayers!

We have seen many different prayers in this book, but here are some very specific ones for those in ministry.

We need to pray they would teach sound doctrine, defend the faith, have boldness, unity, wholesome/edifying speech, be gracious, humble, focused, on task, a hedge of protection, speak with clarity, put on the whole armor of God, and fulfill the great commission.

For those who have been called into full time ministry, we owe it to them to devote time in prayer and supplication on their behalf. They have chosen the road less traveled and we can honor them and honor God by remembering them continually in our prayers.

Choose today to be a prayer warrior for those in God's service.

To Preach/Teach Sound Doctrine and Defend it

Titus 1:9

holding fast the faithful word which is in accordance with the teaching, so that he will be able both to exhort in sound doctrine and to refute those who contradict.

In this day and age where we have instant access to the opinion and thought of every person who chooses to post something on-line, we need to be praying for those in ministry to teach sound Biblical doctrine.   The Bible is a definitive document with truth that needs to be proclaimed.

We also need our leaders to be able to defend against false doctrine and those who want to contradict God's word.   I heard years ago we should be wary of anybody who uses mathematical principles to change God's word.   What do I mean by that?

Addition – people who add to God's word
Subtraction – people who take something away from God's word
Division – people who use God's word to create strife

To Preach the Word at all times

2 Timothy 4:1-2

I solemnly charge you in the presence of God and of Christ Jesus, who is to judge the living and the dead, and by His appearing and His kingdom: preach the word; be ready in season and out of season; reprove, rebuke, exhort, with great patience and instruction.

You never know when an opportunity will present itself to share the Good News of the Gospel of Jesus Christ.   You have to be ready 24/7/365!   Therefore, we need to constantly be lifting our leaders up in prayer so they will be ready for any and every situation they face in a given day.   Each day is like a box of chocolates, you never know what you are going to get.   Some days you only get the chocolate that tastes like it was filled with toothpaste (why do they even put that one in the box).   No matter the day or time, out leaders need to be lifted in prayer to handle all these situations.

Speak with Clarity

Colossians 4:3-4

praying at the same time for us as well, that God will open up to us a door for the word, so that we may speak forth the mystery of Christ, for which I have also been imprisoned; 4 that I may make it clear in the way I ought to speak.

Nothing is worse than listening to a speaker who cannot connect an analogy to the lesson and gets lost as they try to make a point. We used to have a teacher who was a very nice and loving person, but should never have been allowed to speak in front of people. They actually did a disservice to God's word by not being prepared not speaking with clarity.

It takes hard work and preparation to proclaim God's word and those who are called need to be lifted in prayer as they prepare each and every day.

To Use God's Word properly

2 Timothy 3:16-17

All Scripture is inspired by God and profitable for teaching, for reproof, for correction, for training in righteousness; so that the man of God may be adequate, equipped for every good work.

The beauty of God's word is that it is complete! Therefore, we need to pray for our leaders to use it in the right way, with the proper context and references. We need to pray they are using God's word to prepare themselves for their given task – preaching, teaching, making disciples, praying, etc.

Anyone who proclaims God's word will be held to a higher level of accountability and judgment by God.

James 3:1

Let not many of you become teachers, my brethren, knowing that as such we will incur a stricter judgment.

Boldness

Ephesians 6:19

and pray on my behalf, that utterance may be given to me in the opening of my mouth, to make known with boldness the mystery of the gospel,

Boldness is an attribute every Biblical leader should possess. The opposite of boldness is fear or timidity. We know fear does not come from God. Therefore we should be lifting our leaders in prayer so they can boldly proclaim God's word. We need to pray God will give the Power and Love and Discipline!!

2 Timothy 1:7

For God has not given us a spirit of timidity (or cowardice/fear), *but of power and love and discipline.*

Unity

1 Corinthians 1:10

Now I exhort you, brethren, by the name of our Lord Jesus Christ, that you all agree and that there be no divisions among you, but that you be made complete in the same mind and in the same judgment.

Disunity within an organization can bring it crashing down or bring it to a grinding halt. Praying for unity is a powerful prayer our leaders need and desire. They are constantly dealing with human egos and emotions and need the wisdom and discernment necessary to keep unity within their congregations and teams.

Wholesome Speech

Ephesians 4:29

Let no unwholesome word proceed from your mouth, but only such a word as is good for edification according to the need of the moment, so that it will give grace to those who hear.

We need to pray for this wholesome and edifying speech from our leaders. They have the power to build up or tear down and the difference some days may be the amount of prayer we are pouring into their lives. We should also be edifying and encouraging them on a regular basis. You should take the opportunity to send them a quick message of encouragement each week as you are praying for them. It might just be the only encouragement they receive that week.

Graciousness and Salt

Colossians 4:6

Let your speech always be with grace, as though seasoned with salt, so that you will know how you should respond to each person.

As Christians, we never have the right to be unkind or ungracious. However, the only way we can live this out is through the power of Christ in life. We are all frail and weak at times and need to prayer and supplication to lift us up. Our leaders are no different, so we should be lifting them regularly in prayer to be the salt in life.

Humility

Romans 12:3

For through the grace given to me I say to everyone among you not to think more highly of himself than he ought to think; but to think so as to have sound judgment, as God has allotted to each a measure of faith.

The opposite of humility is arrogance. We have all seen arrogance in life and it quickly turns people off to the message that is being delivered. Humility is admitting you do not have all the answers and need from others to complete the task. Humility breaks down barriers and invites other in.

Our leaders need a humble spirit combined with wisdom and discernment.

Focus on the Task

Matthew 9:37-38

Then He *said to His disciples, "The harvest is plentiful, but the workers are few. Therefore beseech the Lord of the harvest to send out workers into His harvest."

It is easy to lose focus over the long haul. A sprint is much easier than a marathon. Almost anybody can sprint for a few seconds, but only a few can run a marathon to the finish. Endurance is needed to keep going to head out into the field for the harvest. Pray for these workers as head into the fields where God has planted them.

Hedge of Protection

Thessalonians 3:1-3

Finally, brethren, pray for us that the word of the Lord will spread rapidly and be glorified, just as it did also with you; and that we will be rescued from perverse and evil men; for not all have faith. But the Lord is faithful, and He will strengthen and protect you from the evil one.

Our leaders need a constant hedge of protection in their life. They are under continually attack and therefore we should have them continually bathed in prayer. The Bible teaches us in 1 Thessalonians that we should pray without ceasing. In these prayers, we should be lifting up prayers of protection for our leaders all the time!

Go, Make, Baptize, Teach

Matthew 28:19-20

Go therefore and make disciples of all the nations, baptizing them in the name of the Father and the Son and the Holy Spirit, teaching them to observe all that I commanded you; and lo, I am with you always, even to the end of the age."

Most Christians know this as the great commission. We should be lifting our leaders up in prayer daily as they work to fulfill the great commission.

The Armor of God

Ephesians 6:10-20

Finally, be strong in the Lord and in the strength of His might. Put on the full armor of God, so that you will be able to stand firm against the schemes of the devil. For our struggle is not against flesh and blood, but against the rulers, against the powers, against the world forces of this darkness, against the spiritual forces of wickedness in the heavenly places. Therefore, take up the full armor of God, so that you will be able to resist in the evil day, and having done everything, to stand firm. Stand firm therefore, having girded your loins with truth, and having put on the breastplate of righteousness, and having shod your feet with the preparation of the gospel of peace; in addition to all, taking up the shield of faith with which you will be able to extinguish all the flaming arrows of the evil one. And take the helmet of salvation, and the sword of the Spirit, which is the word of God.

With all prayer and petition pray at all times in the Spirit, and with this in view, be on the alert with all perseverance and petition for all the saints, and pray on my behalf, that utterance may be given to me in the opening of my mouth, to make known with boldness the mystery of the gospel, for which I am an ambassador in chains; that in proclaiming it I may speak boldly, as I ought to speak.

We would not expect a warrior to head into battle without preparation, armor or weapons. Neither should we expect this from our leaders either. We need to pray the full armor of God upon our leaders each day so they are dressed and ready for the fights that will come. It is not a matter of "if" they need this armor, but a matter of them putting on the armor each day. We can help by bathing them in prayer.

Think of it this way, all of the armor protects the front of their body. They are expected to wade into battle. Who will have their back? We will have their back through prayer! It is on our knees where we will help fight the battle alongside our leaders and missionaries.

Final Thoughts

First, thank you so much for taking the time to read this book. It is my prayer that this has been a blessing to you and your family.

Secondly, if you have an opportunity to send me an e-mail with your thoughts, comments or suggestions, that would be very helpful.

Finally, I hope you were encouraged and strengthened by what you read.

paulbeersdorf@gmail.com

Blessings to you and your family!

Paul Beersdorf

Study Group Lessons

It was my desire to include an 8 week study guide for groups who wanted to dig a little deeper together and share some of their thoughts, ideas and perhaps even provide some accountability.

Please use these weekly lesson plans as a starting point for choosing to make positive changes in your prayer life. While they are designed to be used as a group, you can also go through this by yourself as well.

Remember, you will only get as much out of these lessons as you put into them. Please choose to be open, honest and willing to listen to the thoughts and comments from others.

The idea is to read a chapter or set of chapters each week and then come prepared to answer the questions as a group. Most of the questions are not designed to be easy. Expect to be challenged and to be forced to think about your answers.

Lesson 1
George & God's Concern

Scripture Memory Verse:

Philippians 4:6

Be anxious for nothing, but in everything by prayer and supplication with thanksgiving let your requests be made known to God.

Q. – Why did you choose to read this book?

Q. – What were the key points you got out of these two chapters?

Q. – Do you believe God is concerned about you? Explain your answer

Q. – What do you think about George Mueller? Why do you think he choose not to tell others about his prayers?

Q. – Why do some people only pray in an emergency?

Q. – Why do you think the Bible mentions Gods concern for a sparrow? Why choose a sparrow as an example?

Next Steps

Take time this week to read more about George Mueller and his life and ministry. Also take time to thank God for His concern and make thankfulness a daily part of your prayer routine.

Lesson 2

Being the Answer &
Answered Prayer

Scripture Memory Verse:

<u>Philippians 4:6</u>

Be anxious for nothing, but in everything by prayer and supplication with thanksgiving let your requests be made known to God.

Q. – What were the key points you got out of these chapters?

Q. – Have you had the opportunity to be the answer to a prayer? Explain.

Q. – Have you had specific prayers answered? Explain

Q. – What happened to your faith and trust in God when you were either the answer to the prayer or had a prayer answered?

Q. – When you had prayer answered, did you share this with others? Why? What was their reaction?

Q. – Do you believe God wants to answer your prayers?

Q. – Is it better to be an answer to a prayer or have one answered?

Next Steps

Pray this week that God would actively use you to be an answer to another's prayer.

Lesson 3
Continual Prayer

Scripture Memory Verse:

__1 Thessalonians 5:16-18__

Rejoice always; pray without ceasing; in everything give thanks; for this is God's will for you in Christ Jesus.

Q. – What were the key points you got out of this chapter?

Q. – Do you have a prayer journal? If not, why not?

Q. – How often should you pray for yourself and your family? Explain

Q. – Who should you be praying for on a continual basis?

Q. – When should you stop praying?

Q. – Do you believe prayer will make a difference?

Q. – Should you pray for things that may not come to fruition for years (even decades)? e.g. – your young children's future spouse

Next Steps

Make a list of all your most important relationships (by name) and pray diligently for each and every one of them daily for a week.

Lesson 4
Why, When, Where, Posture

Scripture Memory Verse:

<u>1 Thessalonians 5:16-18</u>

Rejoice always; pray without ceasing; in everything give thanks; for this is God's will for you in Christ Jesus.

Q. – What were the key points you got out of these chapters?

Q. – Why should we pray?

Q. – When should we pray?   Does it matter? Why?

Q. – Where should we pray?   Does it matter? Is one place better than another? Why?

Q. – What is the proper posture of prayer?

Q. –When it comes to prayer, what is God most concerned with?

Q. – Is there ever a bad time to pray?

Next Steps

Choose this week to intentionally pray in different places, at different times, and in different postures.

Lesson 5

A.C.T.S.

Scripture Memory Verse:

<u>1 John 1:9-10</u>

If we confess our sins, He is faithful and righteous to forgive us our sins and to cleanse us from all unrighteousness. If we say that we have not sinned, we make Him a liar and His word is not in us.

Q. – What were the key points you got out of this chapter?

Q. – Do you currently have a method prayer? Explain

Q. – What are the benefits of using this method?

Q. – What do you think is the hardest part of this method? Why?

Q. – Do you have a set time each day to pray? If not, why not? What is keeping you from having a set time each day?

Q. – Why is confession so important?

Q. – What does it mean to have a thankful attitude?

Q. – What are you thankful for?

Next Steps

Use the A.C.T.S. method of praying for 1 week and write your thoughts on how this worked for you. Study the Psalms and learn how the writers praised and honored God. Finally, make a list of everything you are thankful for today.

Lesson 6
Types of Prayer

Scripture Memory Verse:

Matthew 18:19-20

"Again I say to you, that if two of you agree on earth about anything that they may ask, it shall be done for them by My Father who is in heaven. For where two or three have gathered together in My name, I am there in their midst.

Q. – What were the key points you got out of this chapter?

Q. – Which type of prayer do you use most often? Why?

Q. – Do you feel intimidated to pray in public? Why?

Q. – Do you consistently pray with family and friends? What are the benefits of praying with others?

Q. – What does it mean to be a prayer warrior? Explain.

Next Steps

Make a list of all the prayers listed in the chapter and look for opportunities this coming week to use each type of prayer. Seek out a prayer warrior in your church or community and get wise counsel from them on praying.

Lesson 7
Barriers to Prayer

Scripture Memory Verse:

<u>Philippians 2:3</u>

Do nothing from selfishness or empty conceit, but with humility of mind regard one another as more important than yourselves;.

Q. – What were the key points you got out of this chapter?

Q. – Why is humility so important when it comes to preventing barriers to prayer?

Q. – Which of these barriers is the hardest for you to overcome? Why?

Q. – Are you prepared to work and knock these barriers down if they exist in your life? How will you do that? Who will you go to for help?

Q. – What does it mean to be grateful? How can we show gratitude to God?

Q. – What happens in our life when we have unresolved conflict? Why is this so unhealthy?

Next Steps

Pray this week for humility and wisdom! It is harder than it sounds.

Lesson 8
Paul's Call to Prayer

Scripture Memory Verse:

2 Corinthians 1:3-4

Blessed be the God and Father of our Lord Jesus Christ, the Father of mercies and God of all comfort, who comforts us in all our affliction so that we will be able to comfort those who are in any affliction with the comfort with which we ourselves are comforted by God.

Q. – What were the key points you got out of this chapter?

Q. – What is the difference between sympathy and empathy? Which is more important?

Q. – Why is perseverance so important? What happens when you exhibit perseverance?

Q. – What happens when you do not have unity in your life?

Q. – How can wisdom and knowledge help you in your walk with God?

Q. – Why did Paul emphasize seeking God's will?

Q. – What part does LOVE play in prayer?

Next Steps

Memorize the Romans Road and pray for opportunities to share the Good News of the Gospel of Jesus Christ..

Lesson 9

Jesus as the Example

Scripture Memory Verse:

<u>1 John 2:1</u>

My little children, I am writing these things to you so that you may not sin. And if anyone sins, we have an Advocate with the Father, Jesus Christ the righteous;

Q. – What were the key points you got out of this chapter?

Q. – What part did obedience play in His prayers?

Q. – Why do you think so many of the places He prayed were in isolated places?

Q. – How important is it to consider the situation and circumstances when offering prayer?

Q. – Why do you think Jesus took the time to ask God to forgive them for their ignorance as he was dying on the cross?

Q. – How does it make you feel knowing that Jesus is at the right hand of the Father as our advocate?

Q. – What is an advocate? Do you know an advocate? Are you an advocate for anyone?

Next Steps

Take the time this week to think about how you can be an advocate for others. Pray this week that God would give you the opportunity to be an advocate and then thank Him in remembrance for being our advocate.

Lesson 10
Perfect Prayer

Scripture Memory Verse:

<u>2 Timothy 3:16</u>

All Scripture is inspired by God and profitable for teaching, for reproof, for correction, for training in righteousness;

Q. – What were the key points you got out of this chapter?

Q. – Why do so many believe this is the perfect prayer?

Q. – What are the three parts of the prayer? Why is each important?

Q. – Why was it important for Jesus to teach them how to pray?

Q. – Which part of the prayer do you think is most important?

Q. – How important is it to memorize scripture?

Q. – What part does thankfulness play?

Next Steps

Study Matthew chapters 5-8 – the entire sermon on the mount. Take notes and see how prayer fits into the entire message Jesus delivered.

Lesson 11

How not to Pray

Scripture Memory Verse:

<u>James 4:3</u>

You ask and do not receive, because you ask with wrong motives, so that you may spend it on your pleasures.

Q. – What were the key points you got out of this chapter?

Q. – What does the condition of your heart have to do with these issues ?

Q. – Do you think humility can help with any of these issues? Why?

Q. – Which of these issues is the hardest to overcome? Why?

Q. – Which of these issues is the easiest to overcome? Why?

Q. – How can you guard against these issues in your prayer life?

Q. – How many of these issues are within your control?

Next Steps

Consider carefully your motives this week as you pray. Be honest with yourself and with God.   He knows anyway!

Lesson 12
Asking & Fasting

Scripture Memory Verse:

Matthew 7:7

"Ask, and it will be given to you; seek, and you will find; knock, and it will be opened to you.

Q. – What were the key points you got out of these chapters?

Q. – How important is the motive of your heart when you ask?

Q. – Why fast?

Q. – Do you believe God is a good Father and has our best interest in mind when we come to Him in prayer? How would a good father consider each request?

Q. – What will you do (or what have you done) when the answer from God is clearly NO?

Q. – How would your life be different today if He answered YES to all of your prayers? What experiences, relationships and opportunities would be different?

Next Steps

Make a list of all the things you want to bring to God in prayer this week. When you complete your list, consider how many are for yourself and how many are for others. Be prepared for yourself to be that answer to a prayer!

www.ingramcontent.com/pod-product-compliance
Lightning Source LLC
Chambersburg PA
CBHW071538040426
42452CB00008B/1058